Steven F. Dansky

Nobody's Children
Orphans of the HIV Epidemic

*Pre-publication
REVIEWS,
COMMENTARIES,
EVALUATIONS . . .*

"**T**he silent victims of the AIDS pandemic are the children orphaned by their parents' tragic deaths. Dansky provides important information and poignantly depicts these youngster's struggle to survive. This book is professionally sound, moving, and useful for both professionals and interested readers alike."

Ellen Grace Friedman, ACSW
*Associate Director of Support
Services, Methadone Maintenance
Treatment Program, Beth Israel
Medical Center; Associate
Adjunct Professor, New York
University School of Social Work*

More pre-publication
REVIEWS, COMMENTARIES, EVALUATIONS . . .

"*Nobody's Children* is a compelling book, a plea for compassion and understanding for those caught in the multiple epidemics of AIDS, drug addiction, homophobia, domestic violence, and intolerance. Dansky persuades us that these are our people, every orphan, addict, and homosexual. He pushes us to understand the dignity and courage of those who struggle against addiction, death, and prejudice. He is able to put a human face on the voluminous facts and statistics he has gathered with poignant portraits of women, children, and families who protect the orphans, trying to give life in the face of death and dying.

Dansky is especially sensitive to the plight of women and children who are the forgotten participants in the AIDS epidemic and often receive second-class medical treatment. His discussion of the impact of abandonment and loss for children is important and first rate. AIDS has *not* gone away and the epidemic continues to challenge our humanity and sense of community. This is a book for everyone."

Lyn Meehan, CSW
Clinical Supervisor,
Department of Psychiatry,
Bronx Lebanon Hospital Center,
New York

Harrington Park Press
An Imprint of The Haworth Press, Inc.

Nobody's Children
Orphans of the HIV Epidemic

HAWORTH Social Work Practice
Carlton E. Munson, DSW, Senior Editor

New, Recent, and Forthcoming Titles:

Nobody's Children
Orphans of the HIV Epidemic

Steven F. Dansky

Harrington Park Press
An Imprint of The Haworth Press, Inc.
New York • London

Published by

Harrington Park Press, an imprint of The Haworth Press, Inc., 10 Alice Street, Binghamton, NY 13904-1580

Cover design by Marylouise E. Doyle

Library of Congress Cataloging-in-Publication Data

Dansky, Steven.
    Nobody's children : orphans of the HIV epidemic / Steven F. Dansky.
        p.   cm.
    Includes bibliographical references and index.
    ISBN 1-56023-923-9 (alk. paper).
    1. Orphans–United States. 2. Children of AIDS patients–United States. 3. Adoption–United States. I. Title.
HV983.D36 1997
305.9'06945–dc21   96-48940
                                                              CIP

This book is dedicated
to the memory of

James T. Clifford
and
Sandy Gutilla

And for the children
Amy, Blake, Danielle, Erica, Gabriella, Justin,
Kenneth, Sheri, and Zachary

ABOUT THE AUTHOR

Steven F. Dansky, CSW, is a long-time political activist and writer. During the early 1960s, he protested against the war in Vietnam, was a community organizer on New York City's Lower East End, and co-owned the I-Kon bookstore and magazine. In 1969, as a member of the Gay Liberation Front (GLF), he was a founder of the modern gay liberation newspaper, *Come Out!*, which published his theoretical essay "Hey Man," an article widely reprinted in many countries. Dansky also published *Faggotry*, a gay journal of poetry and articles. As a profeminist, he founded the Effeminist Movement and co-published *Double-F: A Magazine of Effeminism.* He is author of *Now Dare Everything: Tales of HIV-Related Psychotherapy* (The Haworth Press, Inc., 1994).

Driven by the HIV pandemic, Dansky volunteered with Gay Men's Health Crisis (GMHC) for eight years, supervised peer group facilitators for Body Positive, and was the therapist of PWA groups for the AIDS Center of Queens County (ACQC). Dansky currently has a private psychotherapy practice in New York City.

CONTENTS

Preface

Sexuality is a part of our behavior. It's part of our world freedom. Sexuality is something that we ourselves create. It is our own creation, and much more than the discovery of a secret side of our desire. We have to understand that with our desires go new forms of relationships, new forms of love, new forms of creation. Sex is not a fatality; it's a possibility for creative life. It's not enough to affirm that we are gay but we must also create a gay life.

Michel Foucault,
"Sex, Power and the Politics of Identity,"
The Advocate, October, 1982

Center Kids, an organization founded to provide services and a haven and community for lesbian and gay parents, is part of the Lesbian and Gay Community Center located in New York City's Greenwich Village. The Lesbian and Gay Community Center is an extraordinary achievement, housing a range of organizations and activities, from anonymous 12-step programs for substance use recovery; to HIV-related organizations such as ACT UP and Body Positive; to the Community Health Project, which is a sexually transmitted disease (STD) walk-in clinic providing health care for HIV/AIDS early assessment and treatment; to ballroom dancing.

Douglas arranged for us to meet after a Center Kids meeting on a late autumn, Sunday afternoon. He was about five-foot-six and had a deep baritone voice that initially seemed incongruous with his stature, but after a while matched the persona of this powerful man. We stopped for some coffee and then walked toward the pier by the Hudson River. We sat looking at New York's bay, which was unusually busy that afternoon. The bow of a luxury liner was silhouetted against the Statue of Liberty, accompanied by several tugboats guiding the ship to a West Side pier to dock.

Douglas adopted a six-month-old child orphaned when his mother died of HIV disease three years ago. He explained, "I never met Joseph's mother, but he was born when she was in an advanced stage of the disease. Of course, Joseph was born with the antibodies to the HIV virus, and I didn't know whether he would be healthy." The first 18 months of an infant's life, when the immune system is developing, is a critical time for children born of HIV-infected mothers. In that window of time the infant will either retain the antibodies to the virus and during the course of early life develop HIV disease, or the infant will throw off the antibodies and be HIV negative. Approximately 30 percent of these infants will develop HIV disease.

Joseph's mother was homeless during her pregnancy and actively using a myriad of substances from alcohol to crack. During a hospitalization for detoxification, she was enrolled in an HIV Women's Project and received some services, including prenatal care. She remained off drugs for the duration of her pregnancy, and when the child was born she made *permanency plans*, the term used for arranging for a guardian to assume parenting, for her infant.

"I never thought I'd be a parent," Douglas continued. "I had been taking care of so many friends stricken with HIV. I lost two partners from the disease. My life was about death. Through a friend, I met a lesbian couple who were about to have a biological child. My friend was the sperm donor. The experience of meeting them stayed in the back of my mind for weeks. And then, as if instantaneously, the thought of adoption preoccupied me.

"Actually several years previous to this event, Eugene, my partner, and I talked about having a child. Eugene was diagnosed HIV positive after we had been together for six years. We decided not to proceed because of the complexities we envisioned for the future. I had already passed psychological tests, physical examinations, and a criminal background check. But adoption seemed out of the question. We gave up the dream to be part of the future, the so-called nontraditional family, raising a child.

"Child care was always a reality of my life. I grew up in rural South Carolina—we were a large family. I was the eldest of five siblings. The African-American family is constantly under assault for being dysfunctional, but we took care of each other, not just our nuclear family, but a large extended one, so I helped raise nephews and nieces and my siblings.

"When I moved to New York, I became involved with child care through one of my friends, a political colleague who was a self-identified gay male, heterosexually married parent. I was committed in theory to day-to-day child care, but I had not assumed any responsibility. The turning point came when Daryl's father and I stayed together from early evening into morning nursing him through the flu. Daryl was an infant at the time, and I remember vomit and feces, and changing linen diaper after diaper—there were no disposables at the time. I yearned to be involved with Daryl's care after that night, and what I had previously thought of as diversion was transformed into something different. Although I had always taken delight in children, I never assumed making a commitment—it was theory. It was a milestone in my life, and I learned how to be capable of taking care of another human being.

"I subscribed to the early feminist doctrine that the personal is political, and the opportunity to put my practice on the line came the following week after a stormy protest by feminists against *Playboy* with Daryl's mother in the front lines. Daryl's mother and father and I began to concretize a child care schedule. We called for a summit meeting, and, sitting at a round Victorian oak table with our date books open, we negotiated terms of a contract. I agreed to two days a week, which included the entire day from Daryl's awakening through preparing him for bed. I realized almost immediately that the schedule constituted 80 percent more time than the average American father spends with his children. It was an opportunity to support my friends, one a feminist, the other a profeminist. Unbeknownst to me at the time, the experience would forever change my life.

"Daryl was 16 months old when I first spent a day alone with him. After he was dressed, we walked through the den, and he pointed at an expressionist painting hanging over the fireplace, saying, 'Whas tha? Whas tha?' I'd answer, 'vermilion,' or 'turquoise,' or 'orange-yellow.' He laughed so vigorously that his body trembled with delight. It was the beginning of our relationship. We played the painting game every day for over a year until he verbalized the colors without help—even recreated them with finger paints splashed on faded paper.

"Daryl was also around other profeminist men, and when we formed a consciousness-raising group, he sat with us through endless meetings. The group sat in a circle on the floor, gazing at the smoldering ashes in a marble fireplace. Daryl climbed over each of us. When each member's turn to speak came, it was shown by tossing a poker chip. Daryl, about eight months old, and at the serious crawling phase, became fascinated with the chips. The group formed at the onset of the AIDS epidemic, but within the first year, one member was diagnosed with gay-related immune deficiency (GRID), the homophobic name mistakenly given before the disease was seen commonly among heterosexuals. Daryl jumped onto the pile of chips, completely disrupting the meeting, and no one knew whose turn it was to speak. It didn't matter.

"When we walked through the streets of New York, Daryl was always snug against my side, bouncing in a yellow canvas sling. In the early 1980s, a male with a child attracted attention, and I remember feeling both embarrassment and self-aggrandizement. On a spring day in New York's lower East Side Stuyvesant Park, Daryl and I watched tulips being planted in orderly rows around a fountain. An ornate wrought-iron fence, a classic design of faggot sticks bound by cable, surrounded the park. I thought, with Daryl on my knee drinking apple juice from a bottle, that masculinity itself was at cross-purposes with child-raising because men are not socialized, overall, to be nurturing. There were times I experienced child care as ego-assaulting. I had to regard the needs of another human being beyond my own who, at least in infancy, is life-dependent. An infant doesn't express him or herself verbally, and so demands perfect and consistent attunement. This was a new experience for me. Surely, I witnessed the milestones of development that brought wonderment and joy, such as the first steps, or the utterance of intelligible words, but I was present for daily caregiving. One evening as Daryl was taking a bath, blowing Pustefix rainbow bubbles against the wall, he reached into the soapy tub water to retrieve a plastic, fluorescent-colored animal float. It was a cobalt blue seahorse. The male of that species, dissimilar from ours, cares for its offspring. Daryl burst out, 'You're Douglas Seahorse.'"

The sun was setting, and I expressed my wish to meet Douglas's son Joseph. Douglas told me that he would be bringing him to the next meeting of Center Kids, and I could meet him then. We parted a few blocks from the pier, and I knew hope was possible even during the most despairing of times.

Acknowledgments

I would like to acknowledge the support from friends without whom this book could not have been written: Chester Chappell, Lynn Friedman, Donna Bersch, John Knoebel, Doug Robinson, Michael Elsasser, and Sally H. Levy.

And to the colleagues whose work has made changes in the lives of people affected during the HIV pandemic: David Altarac, Barbara Agatstein, Kathryn Anastos, Kathy Bell, Maria Bellaflores, Rebecca Farver, Katherine Gold, Christina Hing, Renee Shanker, Joy Silber, Frank Yuen, and Wendy Walker.

Introduction

We're all going to go crazy, living this epidemic every minute,
while the rest of the world goes on out there, all around us, as
if nothing is happening, going on with their own lives and not
knowing what it's like, what we're going through. We're living through war, but where they're living it's peacetime, and
we're all in the same country.

Larry Kramer, *The Normal Heart*

Since the beginning of the human immunodeficiency virus (HIV)
disease pandemic in the United States, children have been orphaned, losing one or both parents. By 1996, the number of orphans
increased to 45,600, and it is predicted to reach between 82,000 and
125,000 orphans by the year 2000. During the present decade,
orphans of the epidemic will need to be cared for by family members, caring adults, or extended family members—or placed in foster
care. Globally, by the year 2000, there will be 40 million HIV-
infected people, of which 10 million will be children. If the gender
ratios remain constant, more than 15 million females and 25 million
males will have HIV infection. There will be approximately ten
million AIDS orphans—children whose parents have died of AIDS—
worldwide. These orphaned children, three-fourths of them not infected with HIV, will require care, financially and socially. The
orphans will need counseling, and their new families, which may
have doubled in size, will often require temporary financial and
housing support.

The first decade of the HIV epidemic concentrated on health care
and ancillary services for individuals with HIV disease. The focus
shifted to families during the 1990s as women became the fastest-
growing segment of the population infected with HIV disease. During the 1990s—the second decade of the epidemic—the mortality

1

rate for women tripled. The Centers for Disease Control and Prevention (CDC) reported that from 1991 to 1992 the number of new cases among women increased 10 percent compared with 2.5 percent for men, making the epidemic solidly associated with women. In 1993, HIV disease ranked as the fourth leading cause of death nationally among women aged 25 to 44, making it a major cause of illness and death among women of childbearing age. The most striking impact of HIV disease can be seen among young women of color, ages 15 to 44: it is the leading cause of death.

In 1995, 17 percent of U.S. children and 12 percent of U.S. adolescents whose mothers died lost them to HIV disease. More than 80 percent of all youth whose mothers have died or will die of HIV disease (an estimated 36,560 youth) are offspring of African Americans or Latinas.[1]

Besides the thousands of children orphaned when their mothers or fathers die of HIV disease, are the children who have HIV disease themselves. The estimated national prevalence of HIV infection among childbearing women was 1.7 HIV-infected women per 1,000 childbearing women.[2] Approximately 7,000 HIV-infected women gave birth every year from 1989 to 1992. Assuming a 15 to 30 percent perinatal transmission rate, about 1,000 to 2,000 HIV-infected infants were born in each of those years.

The connection between HIV and substance use is inarguable and includes direct transmission through shared needle use, unprotected sexual activity with an HIV-infected substance user, and unprotected sexual activity under the influence of crack cocaine, alcohol, or other substances. Communities all across the United States are struggling to confront the twin epidemics of HIV and substance use. Approximately 31 percent of all HIV disease cases relate either directly or indirectly to intravenous drug use. Among women, 30 percent were infected through injection drug use and 36 percent through heterosexual contact with an HIV-positive male. Lack of substance use treatment slots, inadequate training, and limited funding only perpetuate this insidious link, with drug treatment centers unable to accommodate the growing numbers of substance users with HIV disease.

More than 5 percent of the 4 million women who gave birth in the United States in 1992 used illegal drugs while they were pregnant. A government survey gathered self-report data from a national sample of 2,613 women who delivered babies in 52 urban and rural hospitals during 1992. Based on these data, an estimated 221,000 women who gave birth in 1992 used illicit drugs while they were pregnant. Marijuana and cocaine were the most frequently used illicit drugs–2.9 percent, or 119,000 women, used marijuana, and another 1.1 percent, or 45,000 women, used cocaine at some time during their pregnancy.[3]

Approximately 70 percent of all pediatric HIV cases occur as a result of maternal exposure to HIV through intravenous drug use or sex with an intravenous drug user. In 1994, pediatric cases of HIV disease increased 18 percent from the previous year. Many more children are HIV infected, but have not progressed to the full-blown disease. In 1991, HIV infection was the second leading cause of death among African-American children ages one to four years in New Jersey, Massachusetts, New York, and Florida. Almost 60 percent of pediatric cases of HIV disease occurs in children of color–39 percent African American, 18 percent Latino, .7 percent Asian or Pacific Islander, and .3 percent Native American.

Increasingly, parents who are themselves infected must make agonizing choices for themselves, their infected children, and their uninfected children. These parents may sacrifice their own health as they seek care for their children and must struggle with issues of how to provide for both sick and healthy children after their death. In New York City, officials predict an orphan burden of approximately 20,000 children, of whom about one-fourth are HIV positive.

HIV-infected women, indeed all women, must have access to treatment and health care. Additionally, women, particularly women of color, have traditionally experienced difficulty qualifying for clinical trials. For a parent whose child is diagnosed with HIV disease and whose only hope lies in the child's participation in an HIV disease-related clinical trial, the exclusion of children from trials highlights one of the inequities of research programs. Children should be included in HIV disease-related clinical trials with parents and patient advocates participating in decisions about the care of children.

While some ill HIV-infected women establish future custody plans for their children, most do not. Lack of planning stems from denial, fear of disclosure, lack of a potential guardian, lack of any formal counseling or legal advice, and inflexible laws. Not infrequently, elderly grandmothers in ill health become guardians by default when the mothers die. The health care team, with the assistance of legal counsel, should discuss future custody plans with every HIV-infected parent. Every state should review its existing guardianship laws, many of which leave children in legal limbo at the time of a parent's death, even when a guardian has been named in the parent's will. One solution to prevent such limbo is the Stand-By Guardianship Law, enacted in New York in 1992, which allows an ill or dying woman to name a guardian for her children prior to mental incapacitation, physical debilitation, or death.

About half of parents die before they designate guardians to assume custody of their children. The Stand-By Guardianship Law, enacted in Illinois and New York, allows parents to name a standby guardian to care for their children on a temporary basis. Parents with HIV disease do not have to give up custody every time they go into the hospital, and they can know who will take in their children after they die. In 1995, over 425,000 infants were exposed to drugs, and a significant number will require foster or adoptive families. Most of them, living in that complex place called poverty, have a whole range of unmet social, educational, and health needs. Many have already experienced a variety of personal losses unrelated to HIV disease. These orphans are themselves at high risk for HIV infection because of early sexual activity, unsafe sexual practices, and experimentation with drugs. Many of these children who experience the loss of a parent from HIV disease also witness the illness and death of one or more infected siblings.

When a family member dies, children react differently than adults. Preschool children usually see death as temporary and reversible—a belief reinforced by cartoon characters who die and come to life again. Children between the ages of five and nine begin to think more like adults about death, yet they still believe it will never happen to them or anyone they know. In children, grief may manifest in the following ways: an extended period of depression in which the child loses interest in daily activities and events; inability to sleep; loss of appetite; prolonged fear of being alone; acting much younger for an extended period; excessively imitating the dead person; repeated statements of wanting to join the dead person; withdrawal from friends; and a sharp drop in school performance or refusal to attend school. The depressed child may exhibit persistent sadness; an inability to enjoy previously favorite activities; increased activity or irritability; frequent complaints of physical illnesses such as headaches and stomachaches; frequent absences from school or poor performance in school; persistent boredom; low energy; poor concentration; and a major change in eating or sleeping patterns.

Adding to a child's shock and confusion at the death of a brother, sister, or parent is the unavailability of other family members, who may be so shaken by grief that they are unable to cope with the normal responsibility of child care.

Parents should be aware of normal childhood responses to a death in the family, and of danger signals. According to child and adolescent psychiatrists, it is normal during the weeks following the death for some children to feel immediate grief or persist in the belief that the family member is still alive. Long-term denial of the death or avoidance of grief is unhealthy and can later surface in more severe problems. A child who is frightened about attending a funeral should not be forced to go; however, some service or observance is recommended, such as lighting a candle, saying a prayer, or visiting a grave site.

Once children accept the death, they are likely to display their feelings of sadness on and off over a long period, and often at unexpected moments. The surviving relatives should spend as much time as possible with the child, making it clear that the child has permission to show his or her feelings openly or freely.

The person who has died was essential to the stability of the child's world, and anger is a natural reaction. The child may reveal the anger in boisterous play, nightmares, irritability, or a variety of other behaviors. Often he or she will show anger toward the surviving family members. After a parent dies, many children will act younger than they are. The child may temporarily become more infantile, demanding food, attention, and cuddling, and talking "baby talk."

Younger children believe they are the cause of what happens around them. A young child may believe a parent, grandparent, brother, or sister died because he or she had once wished the person dead. The child feels guilty because the wish "came true." These warning signs indicate that professional help may be needed. A child and adolescent psychiatrist can help the child accept the death and assist the survivors in helping the child through the mourning process.

Significant depression probably exists in about 5 percent of children and adolescents in the general population. Not only adults become depressed. Children and teenagers also may have depression. Depression is defined as an illness when it persists. Children who are under stress, who experience loss, or who have attentional, learning, or conduct disorders are at a higher risk for depression. The behavior of depressed children and teenagers differs from the behavior of depressed adults. Child and adolescent psychiatrists advise parents to be aware of signs in their youngsters.

A child who used to play often with friends may now spend most of the time alone and without interests. Things that were once fun now bring little joy to the depressed child. Children and adolescents who are depressed may say they want to be dead or may talk about suicide. Depressed adolescents may abuse alcohol or other drugs as a way to feel better.

Children and adolescents who cause trouble at home or at school may actually be depressed but not know it. Because the youngster may not always seem sad, parents and teachers may not realize that troublesome behavior is a sign of depression. When asked directly, these children can sometimes state they are unhappy or sad.

Early diagnosis and medical treatment are essential for depressed children. For help, parents should ask their physician to refer them to a child and adolescent psychiatrist, who can diagnose and treat depression in children and teenagers.

Ultimately, the majority of HIV-affected children will end up in formal or informal foster care or adoptive care. A variety of innovative foster care programs have been created throughout the country to meet the complex needs of HIV-positive children. Few programs, however, have focused adequately on the needs of uninfected siblings. Special HIV units designed to track and oversee the care of HIV-infected foster children should expand their programs to include all HIV-affected children. Model programs designed to augment early permanency planning are urgently needed. Such programs would train, certify, and supervise a future guardian (typically identified by an ill HIV-infected mother) to provide respite care, home assistance, and other help in caring for HIV-affected children. As the mother becomes more ill, the role of the guardian enlarges as necessary. Ultimately, at the time of maternal debilitation, mental incapacitation, or death, the individual would become either a foster parent or an adoptive parent. As with many of the successful HIV disease programs established to date, such model programs very likely will need to cross traditional boundaries, improve interagency communications, and establish new collaborative relationships.

NOTES

1. D. Michaels and C. Levine, Estimates of the Number of Motherless Youth Orphaned by HIV Disease in the United States. *Journal of the American Medical Association* 1992;268:34–61.

2. National Survey of Childbearing Women, 1992.

3. *NIDA Notes*, January/February, 1995.

Chapter 1

The Second Decade

Both the Moral Majority, who are recycling medieval language to explain AIDS, and those ultra-leftists who attribute AIDS to some sort of conspiracy, have a clearly political analysis of the epidemic. But even if one attributes its cause to a microorganism rather than the wrath of God, or the workings of the CIA, it is clear that the way in which AIDS has been perceived, conceptualized, imagined, researched and financed makes this the most political of diseases.

Dennis Altman, *AIDS in the Mind of America*

The human immunodeficiency virus (HIV) disease or acquired immune deficiency syndrome (AIDS) pandemic dates to 1981 when reports of the first cases of pneumocystis carrini pneumonia (PCP) occurred in the United States. By the end of the first decade of the AIDS epidemic, there were more than 250,000 Americans with HIV disease. From the beginning of the epidemic until 1995, 295,473 individuals died of HIV disease. This is three times more Americans than died in the Vietnam War, or more Americans than died in the Korean and Vietnam wars combined. By 1995, 1,129,810 cumulative AIDS cases in adults and children worldwide had been reported to the United Nations' World Health Organization (WHO) Global Programme on AIDS since the onset of the pandemic, a 20 percent increase in cases from the previous year (Figure 1.1). Allowing for underdiagnosis, incomplete reporting, and reporting delay, and based on the available data on HIV disease, it has been estimated that there are actually over 4.5 million cases of HIV disease globally, with the majority of cases occurring in sub-

9

FIGURE 1.1. Global HIV/AIDS Cases (Cumulative Total = 1,129,810)

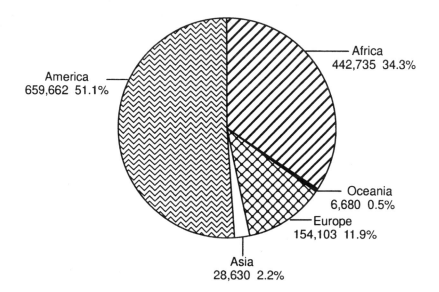

Africa
442,735 34.3%

America
659,662 51.1%

Oceania
6,680 0.5%

Europe
154,103 11.9%

Asia
28,630 2.2%

Source: World Health Organization (WHO), 1995.

Saharan Africa and the Americas (Figures 1.2 and 1.3). As of late 1994, it was estimated that 18 million adults and about 1.5 million children were infected with HIV.[1] In the United States also, the number of reported HIV disease cases does not accurately represent the scope of the epidemic. Reported figures are estimated to represent only 10 to 15 percent of the total number of HIV-infected individuals.

In 1995, the Centers for Disease Control and Prevention (CDC) estimated that approximately one adult male in 100 (1:100) and one adult female in 600 (1:600) was HIV positive, indicating that at least one million people in the United States were HIV infected.

As in previous years, men who have sex with men (either gay-identified or bisexual) account for most of the cases reported each year: men who have sex with men continued to account for the largest proportion of cases, at 44 percent (Figure 1.4). All men represented 82 percent of HIV disease cases reported among adults and adolescents (adolescents are 13 years old or older). The estimated

FIGURE 1.2. Global Reported HIV Cases Versus Estimated HIV Disease by Region

Region	Cumulative AIDS Cases	Estimated Total HIV
Sub-Saharan Africa	210,376	8,000,000+
South/Southeast Asia	1,445	1,500,000+
Latin America and Caribbean	64,048	1,500,000
North America	249,035	1,000,000+
Western Europe	78,049	500,000
North Africa/Middle East	1,160	75,000
Eastern Europe/Central Asia	2,850	50,000
Oceania, including Australia	3,963	25,000+
East Asia/Pacific	663	25,000+
TOTAL	611,589	13,000,000+

Source: United Nations' World Health Organization (WHO), Global Programme on AIDS.

FIGURE 1.3. Global Cumulative AIDS Cases 1979-1995

	Africa	America	Asia	Europe	Oceania	Total
1979	0	2	0	0	0	2
1980	0	187	1	17	0	205
1981	0	509	2	37	0	548
1982	2	1,665	3	117	91	1,878
1983	19	5,017	11	412	97	5,556
1984	206	11,697	19	982	173	13,077
1985	727	24,379	46	2,457	315	27,924
1986	6,165	45,701	132	4,852	567	57,417
1987	23,919	80,263	282	14,492	891	118,947
1988	51,231	127,960	458	25,303	1,489	206,441
1989	92,526	184,162	746	39,658	2,188	319,280
1990	147,054	249,203	1,224	56,969	2,958	457,408
1991	219,810	327,782	2,062	75,906	3,855	629,515
1992	293,441	427,663	4,101	96,603	4,721	826,529
1993	360,656	528,394	11,469	118,656	5,600	1,024,684
1994	426,249	611,869	23,176	142,197	6,506	1,025,073
1995	442,735	659,662	28,630	154,103	6,680	1,291,810
TOTALS	442,735	659,662	28,630	154,103	6,680	1,291,810

Source: WHO, Global Programme on AIDS, January 1994.

FIGURE 1.4. U.S. Adult/Adolescent HIV/AIDS Cases by Exposure Category

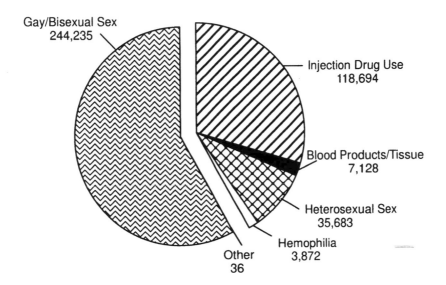

Source: Centers for Disease Control (CDC), *HIV/AIDS Surveillance Report,* 1995.

incidence of HIV disease opportunistic illnesses (OIs), which define so-called full-blown HIV disease, increased 13 percent from 1990 to 1993 among men who have sex with men (Figure 1.5). In 1993, HIV disease was the eighth most common cause of death in the general population and it is expected to become the third by the turn of the century (Figure 1.6).

Despite the greater incidence of HIV disease among males, in several cities it is the most common cause of death in young females, making it a disease that affects the entire family, with mothers, fathers, and children dying, leaving orphans as survivors of what was once a family. HIV-infected women have an increased risk of death, rather than gradual disease progression. Women are one-third more likely to die without an HIV-defining condition than are HIV-infected men.[4]

FIGURE 1.5. U.S. HIV Disease Cases by Single Exposure Categories

Mode of Transmission	Number	Percent
Men who have sex with men	220,470	51%
Injecting drug use	90,644	21%
Hemophilia/coagulation disorder	2,809	1%
Heterosexual contact	30,691	7%
Receipt of transfusion	6,858	2%
Receipt of transplant of tissues/organs or artificial insemination	8	0%
Other	36	0%
Single mode of exposure subtotal	351,516	81%

Source: CDC, HIV/AIDS Surveillance Report, December 1994.

FIGURE 1.6. Ten Leading Causes of Death in the United States

Cause of Death	Number	Death Rate	Percentage of Total Deaths
All Causes	2,268,000	879.3	100.0
1 Heart Disease	739,860	286.9	32.6
2 Cancer	530,870	205.8	23.4
3 Stroke	149,740	58.1	6.6
4 Chronic obstructive lung diseases and allied conditions	101,090	39.2	4.5
5 Accidents and adverse effects	88,630	34.4	3.9
Motor vehicle accidents	40,880	15.9	1.8
All other accidents and adverse effects	47,750	18.5	2.1
6 Pneumonia and influenza	81,730	31.7	3.6
7 Diabetes Mellitus	55,110	21.4	2.4
8 HIV Disease	38,500	14.9	1.7
9 Suicide	31,230	12.1	1.4
10 Homicide and legal intervention	25,470	9.9	1.1

Women's risk of relatively early death suggests consequential factors that correlate to their social status in a male supremacist culture. Access to health care resources, including clinical trials, that focus on relevant medical concerns for women, such as reproductive health and the manifestations of HIV disease in women, have been traditionally restricted, particularly for the poor and women of color. Women are often isolated within the family unit, especially when they are caregivers to other ill members, so that social supports are constricted. This situation is exacerbated when there is domestic violence in the family. Globally, domestic violence, infanticide, sexual abuse, rape, battering, and wife-burning (a practice in some cultures in which a man murders his wife in order to get a higher dowry through another marriage[5]), are several pervasive problems facing women. Improving the delivery of health care to women involves changing the oppressive status of women in our patriarchal society. All women face obstacles to better health care through their absence from clinical drug trials due to social customs that relegate women to the status of reproductive vessels and little else. Consequently, aspects of women's health, including nutrition and aging, responses to illnesses such as HIV disease, and diseases that only affect women, receive nominal attention or funding.

For instance, it was not until 1992–ten years into the epidemic–that the list of conditions set by the CDC to define HIV disease included gynecological symptoms.

> Far too many women seen in primary care and other settings are not being recognized as being at risk of HIV infection, and therefore are not able to benefit from the early medical intervention offered to those who have been diagnosed as HIV-positive. And, many women currently enrolled in primary care settings for treatment of HIV illness, are not receiving appropriate gynecological care.[6]

HIV-infected women are more at risk of developing serious, invasive cervical cancer. Therefore, twice-annual Pap smears are essential to detect squamous cell abnormalities. The diagnosis of human papilloma virus (HPV) is critical because it accounts for a vast majority of genital tract dysplasia. In one study of 300 HIV-positive women, HPV, a common sexually transmitted disease, occurred in up to a quarter of women aged 25 to 35. HPV has been linked to cervical cancer. One in five of them had squamous dysplasia, a precancerous condition. In 1993, the CDC added cervical cancer to its list of HIV disease-related illnesses. Researchers believe that the compromised immune system of HIV-positive women allows HPV to take hold more aggressively, putting them at greater risk of the cancer.

It was women's advocacy groups who forced federal health officials to change the HIV-disease definitions to include invasive cervical cancer. Many advocates reported that infected women had more cervical cancer, but health officials were skeptical. Cervical cancer is a preventable disease, but it requires physicians to perform complete gynecological examinations for women known to be HIV infected and for women who do not know their HIV serostatus.

An examination of women's health care needs exposes some of the most intractable issues endangering women's well-being, which are the least acknowledged threats—domestic violence, the damaging effects of illegal abortion, sexually transmitted diseases, and genital mutilation. Somewhat paradoxically, these issues ultimately have less to do with women's health in and of itself than they have to do with society as a whole. Improving women's health requires a reexamination of sexual and cultural mores: the task of securing women's health must be accomplished within the context of social transformation.

The sanctioning of abuse, overt or implicit, is commonplace, rooted in the social relationship of men and women; it prevents many women from escaping male batterers, and often physicians fail to recognize the extent of the medical problem. Battering may be the leading cause of injury to women in the United States. For American women, between 22 and 35 percent of visits to emergency rooms are for injuries caused by domestic violence.[7] Due to underreporting, statistics on the incidence of domestic violence are unreliable; estimates suggest that in reality, between 20 and more than 50 percent of women throughout the world may be abused. In Papua New Guinea, 56 percent of married women in cities reported battering. Eighteen percent were treated at a hospital because they had been beaten. In Bombay, India, one of four deaths in women between the ages of 15 and 24 is caused by burning.

While women's absence from clinical trials has been acknowledged, it is apparent that women's health concerns, such as breast cancer and menopause, have not been investigated with the same determination as men's health issues. Many studies on illnesses that affect both sexes—

specifically, heart disease and HIV disease–have not scrutinized the etiology or expression of the disorders in women.

Some investigators have looked at prenatal transmission, studying how and when and with what degree of prevalence mothers infect their fetus or infant. (See Figure 1.7.) HIV can be transmitted from an infected woman to her fetus or newborn during pregnancy, through labor or delivery, or after birth through breastfeeding.[8,9,10] Almost one of every four babies born to HIV-infected women will develop HIV disease; 92 percent of pediatric cases occur through perinatal transmission. While HIV transmission to a fetus can occur as early as eight weeks old, accumulating data suggest that at least

FIGURE 1.7. U.S. Pediatric AIDS Cases (Cumulative Total = 6,611)

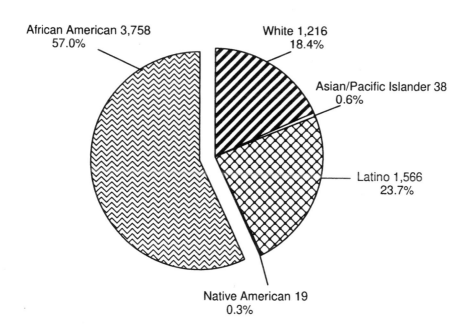

African American 3,758
57.0%

White 1,216
18.4%

Asian/Pacific Islander 38
0.6%

Latino 1,566
23.7%

Native American 19
0.3%

Source: CDC, Surveillance Report, 1995.

half of perinatal transmissions in nonbreastfeeding populations may occur close to or during birth.[11,12] Several studies regarding maternal HIV transmission have been conducted, with preliminary data suggesting factors that increase transmission risk. These factors include the following: (1) low CD4+ counts; (2) high maternal viral titer; (3) advanced HIV disease; (4) presence of p24 antigen in maternal serum; (5) placental membrane inflammation; (6) intrapartum events resulting in increased exposure of the fetus to maternal blood; (7) breastfeeding; (8) premature rupture of membranes; and (9) premature delivery.[13,14,15,16] Cesarean section delivery, the presence of maternal neutralizing antibodies, and maternal zidovudine (AZT) therapy have been associated with a decreased rate of transmission in some studies.[17,18]

Because the search for alternative means of protection against infection through sexual intercourse has only just begun, women remain reliant on men to use condoms. The recently marketed female condom may confer the same degree of protection that the male condom does; it still, however, requires male consent. Only recently have laboratories begun to investigate microbicides that women can administer directly and, if need be, privately. Researchers also hope to find a form of AIDS prevention that could permit pregnancy.

The National Institutes of Health (NIH) conducted a clinical trial designed to evaluate whether zidovudine (AZT) administered to HIV-infected pregnant women and their infants could reduce the rate of transmission from mother to infant. AZT given to HIV-infected women during pregnancy and to their infants for the first six weeks of life can reduce the HIV infection rate in the infants. Vertical transmission of HIV (infection of an infant through exposure to maternal virus during pregnancy or labor and delivery) accounts for the vast majority of HIV infection in infants and children worldwide. In the United States, over 5,000 children have developed AIDS. Approximately 7,000 infants are born to HIV-infected women each year in the United States. Not all infants born to infected women become infected. Vertical transmission rates vary in different regions and different patient populations. The overall transmission rate in the United States is about 20 to 25 percent.

In 1994, the NIH released the following results of the study of AZT and pregnant women with 421 infants born to women enrolled in the trial:

> Of the 364 evaluable infants, 53 had HIV infection. Of those 53, 13 had received zidovudine and 40 had received the placebo. The estimated rate of transmission in the group that received zidovudine is 8.3%, whereas the rate of transmission in the group that received the placebo was 25.5%. These results are statistically significant (p = .00006) and indicate that if zidovudine is used in a similar population, only 8 out of 100 infants will be infected, compared to 25 out of 100 infants when zidovudine is not used. All 53 HIV-infected infants had at least one HIV-positive culture.[19]

Of the women enrolled, 51 percent were African American, 29 percent Hispanic and 0.2 percent Asian. The ethnic and racial distribution of the trial participants is comparable to that in the population of HIV-infected women in the United States.

HIV affects people of all ages. Adolescents face difficulties without effective warning of this new risk to their futures. Adolescents practice many of the same behaviors that put adults at risk. Given the length of time between infection and diagnosis, which can be up to ten years, many adults diagnosed with AIDS in their mid- to late-twenties were infected during adolescence. The language of prevention needs to be concordant with the myriad subcultures and ethnicities of people at risk, instead of imposing constraints in the name of morality. This withholds potentially lifesaving information and devices to avoid offending a public presumed to agree with such constraints. Many people suffer and grieve in private, out of fear of stigma, discrimination, or rejection.

In 1994, young men represented a population at high risk for HIV; among men 20 to 24 years old reported with AIDS, 60 percent reported sex with men. This percentage is higher than the percentage of men who have sex with men among all men reported with AIDS (53 percent). Heterosexual injection drug users and injection drug users who have sex with other men accounted for 24 percent and 6 percent of cases among men, respectively. The proportion of cases among women increased steadily during the past decade.

AIDS among women represented 18 percent of adults and adolescents with AIDS reported in 1994. Among women reported with AIDS in 1994, most were infected with HIV through injection drug use (41 percent) or heterosexual contact with a man who was at risk for or had HIV infection or AIDS (38 percent). Nineteen percent of women with AIDS were reported without risk for HIV exposure. After these cases were followed up by state and local health departments, most women for whom a risk was identified were found to have become infected through heterosexual contact (66 percent) or injection drug use (27 percent). Some cases reported without risk of HIV exposure are likely to represent unrecognized heterosexual transmission. (See Figure 1.8 for current trends and Figure 1.9 for U.S. HIV disease fatalities.)

FIGURE 1.8. Current Trends

- 347,767 cases in males and 53,978 cases in females (four cases were reported with sex not specified)
- 396,015 cases in adults and adolescents and 5,734 cases among children less than 13 years of age
- Decreased from 85 to 83 percent
- The proportion of cases reported among whites decreased from 47 to 43 percent
- The proportion of cases among African Americans increased from 35 to 38 percent
- The proportion of cases among Latinos increased from 15 to 18 percent
- By exposure category, 47 percent were reported among men who have sex with men
- 28 percent were attributed to injecting drug use; 9 percent were attributed to heterosexual contact
- 5 percent were reported among men who have sex with men and inject drugs
- 1 percent were attributed to receipt of blood transfusion, blood components, or tissue
- 1 percent occurred in persons with hemophilia or other coagulation disorder
- 9 percent occurred among persons whose risk has not been identified

Source: Current Trends from the Centers for Disease Control and Prevention.

FIGURE 1.9. U.S. HIV/AIDS Fatalities (Cumulative Total = 295,473)

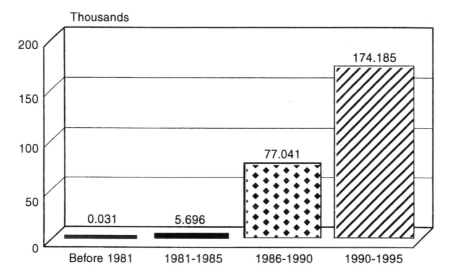

Source: CDC, *Surveillance Report*, 1995.

Most people with HIV infection and AIDS live in big cities, but the number of people developing AIDS in smaller cities, towns, and rural areas is growing. The highest U.S. rates are in the Northeast and in Puerto Rico. Before 1985, more than half of the children with AIDS were from New York City, Newark, and Miami. Currently, however, most children with HIV disease are outside these cities.

AIDS education is seriously needed in rural communities. This includes even the simplest of education about HIV infection for health care providers. Ignorance and misinformation are seriously hampering if not crippling efforts to treat those who are sick, clearly contributing to the rapid increase in rates of HIV infection in rural America, and contributing greatly to the discrimination against and ostracism of people living with HIV disease. Drug education, prevention, and treatment programs range from grossly inadequate to nonexistent.

The disproportionate impact of AIDS on young people is illustrated by the years of potential life lost. Health economists calculated the years of potential life lost before age 65 to describe the extent to which deaths from HIV disease occur primarily in young people. In 1987, the number of years of potential life lost due to HIV disease was 432,000. This figure compared with 246,000 for stroke, 1.5 million for heart disease, and 1.8 million for cancer. While the rates for these other major diseases remain stable, the number of years of potential life lost due to HIV disease continues to increase. In 1991, estimates placed the years of potential life lost due to HIV disease between 1.2 and 1.4 million, ranking it third among all diseases. By 1992, the years of potential life lost due to HIV disease will grow to between 1.5 and 2.1 million.

Disproportionately, and increasingly, the epidemic affects already disadvantaged segments of society, such as communities of color, women, and those struggling with poverty and substance use. HIV disease is increasing among racial and ethnic minority populations. People of all races and ethnic groups have been infected with HIV, but racial and ethnic minority populations have been most disproportionately affected. Through 1992, 47 percent of all reported HIV disease cases occurred among African Americans and Latinos, while these two population groups represent only 21 percent of the total U.S. population. Asians, Pacific Islanders, American Indians, and Alaska Natives account for a small percentage of all reported HIV disease cases. Figures 1.10 and 1.11 show the breakdown of HIV disease cases by race, ethnicity, and gender.

The relative impoverishment of African Americans, Latinos, Native Americans, and many Asian Americans and Pacific Islanders bears testament to the enduring nature of yesterday's burdens, and the difficulty of playing catch-up at a time when the dominant majority is apt to discount matters of race. Racist attitudes remain part of our national social and political life, promoting prejudice and discrimination against people of color and reinforcing social and institutional arrangements that limit opportunities for members of minority communities.

The continuing widespread stigmatization of people of color creates enormous difficulties for effectively combating the HIV/ AIDS epidemic. Perhaps the greatest of these is that communities of color fear that stigmatization and discrimination are likely to increase as the public becomes more aware of the disproportionate number of people of color who are infected with HIV. For these communities,

FIGURE 1.10. U.S. AIDS Cases by Race and Ethnicity for Males (Cumulative Total = 408,874)

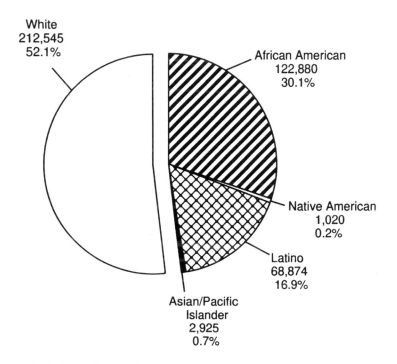

Source: CDC, *Surveillance Report*, 1995.

disproportionate representation raises the fear that they will be saddled with the disease, blamed for it, stigmatized by it, and left to deal with it on their own.

People of color have been affected by the HIV epidemic since its inception. The first report of AIDS in an African-American man was in June 1981. By August 1981, one in nine of the reported homosexual males with AIDS was African American. The first case-series report on women with AIDS, published in April 1982, described five women: three Latinos, one white, and one African American. Indeed, as early as 1982, statistical evidence suggested that the epidemic posed a disproportionately serious problem for African Americans and Latinos, and that most of the people at risk for infection in these groups were of relatively low socioeconomic status.

FIGURE 1.11. U.S. HIV/AIDS Cases by Race and Ethnicity for Females (Cumulative Total = 68,021)

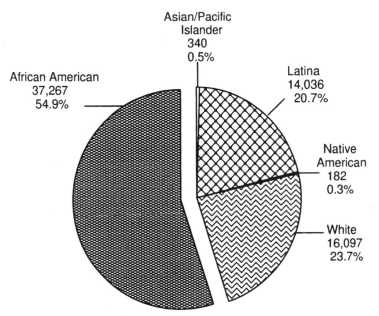

Asian/Pacific
Islander
340
0.5%

Latina
14,036
20.7%

African American
37,267
54.9%

Native
American
182
0.3%

White
16,097
23.7%

Source: CDC, *Surveillance Report*, 1995.

NOTES

1. World Health Organization, Global Programme on AIDS, January 1995.

2. Ibid.

3. National Center for Health Statistics, U.S. Department of Health and Human Services.

4. National Institute of Allergy and Infectious Diseases (NIAID), reported in the December 28 *Journal of the American Medical Association.*

5. M. Holloway, Trends in Women's Health, A Global View. *Scientific American* August 1994:27(2).

6. I. Davis, MD, Preface in Gynecological Care Manual for HIV Positive Women. R. Denenberg, FNP, Essential Medical Systems, 1993.

7. M. Holloway, Trends in Women's Health: A Global View. *Scientific American* August 1994:27(2).

8. S.H. Lewis, C. Reynolds-Kohler, H.E. Fox, and J.A. Nelson. HIV-1 in Trophoblastic and Villous Hofbauer Cells, and Haematological Precursors in Eight-week Fetuses. *Lancet* 1990;335:565-568.

9. L.M. Mofenson and S.M. Wolinsky. Current Insights Regarding Vertical Transmission. In *Pediatric HIV Disease: The Challenge of HIV Infection in Infants, Children, and Adolescents*, 2nd ed. (P.A. Pizzo and C.M. Wilfert, eds.). Baltimore: Williams & Wilkins, 1994:179-203.

10. D.T. Dunn, M.L. Newell, A.E. Ades and C.S. Peckham. Risk of Human Immunodeficiency Virus Type 1 Transmission Through Breastfeeding. *Lancet* 1992;340:585-588.

11. M.F. Rogers, C.Y. Ou, M. Rayfield, P.A. Thomas, E.E. Schoenbaum, E. Abrams, K. Krasinski, P.A. Selwyn, J. Moore, A. Kaul, et al. Use of the Polymerase Chain Reaction for Early Detection of the Proviral Sequences of Human Immunodeficiency Virus in Infants Born to Seropositive Mothers. *New England Journal of Medicine* 1989;320:1649-1654.

12. C. Rouzioux, D. Costagliola, M. Burgard, S. Blanche, M.J. Mayaux, C. Griscelli, and A.J. Valleron. Timing of Mother-to-child HIV-1 transmission Depends on Maternal Status. *HIV Disease* 1993;7 (Supplement 2):S49-S52.

13. R.W. Ryder, W. Nsa, S.E. Hassig, F. Behets, M. Rayfield, B. Ekungola, A.M. Nelson, U. Mulenda, H. Francis, K. Mwandagalirwa, et al. Perinatal Transmission of the Human Immunodeficiency Virus Type I to Infants of Seropositive Women in Zaire. *New England Journal of Medicine* 1989;320:1637-1642.

14. *Op Cit.*

15. M.E. St. Louis, M. Kamenga, C. Brown, A.M. Nelson, T. Manzila, V. Batter, F. Behets, U. Kabagabo, R.W. Ryder, M. Oxtoby, et al. Risk for perinatal HIV-1 transmission according to maternal immunologic, virologic, and placental factors. *Journal of the American Medical Association (JAMA)*, 1993;269:2853-2859.

16. D.N. Burns, S. Landesman, L.R. Muenz, R.P. Nugent, J.J. Goedert, H. Minkoff, J.H. Walsh, H. Mendez, A. Rubinstein, and A. Willoughby. Cigarette smoking, Premature Rupture of Membranes, and Vertical Transmission of HIV-1 Among Women with Low CD4+ Levels. *Journal of Acquired Immune Deficiency Syndrome* 1994;7:718-726.

17. D.T. Dunn, M.L. Newell, M.J. Mayaux, C. Kind, C. Hutto, J.J. Goedert, and W. Andiman. Mode of Delivery and Vertical Transmission of HIV-1: A Review of Prospective Studies. *Journal of Acquired Immune Deficiency Syndrome*, 1994;7:1064-1066.

18. G. Scarlatti, J. Albert, P. Rossi, et al., Mother-to-Child Transmission of Human Immunodeficiency Virus Type 1: Correlation with Neutralizing Antibodies Against Primary Isolates. *Journal of Infectious Diseases* 1993;168:207-210.

19. Press Release, National Institutes of Health, National Institute of Allergy and Infectious Diseases, February 20, 1994.

20. National Commission on AIDS, Washington, DC, December 1992.

Chapter 2

The State of the Child

AIDS occupies such a large part in our awareness because of
what it has been taken to represent. It seems the very model of
all the catastrophes privileged populations feel await them.

Susan Sontag, *AIDS and Its Metaphors*

The epidemics of HIV disease and substance use, in particular
cocaine and its inexpensive street-sale derivative crack, function in
tandem by decimating entire segments of the population. In 1991,
the U.S. Department of Health and Human Services reported that
22,000 so-called *boarder babies* were abandoned in 851 hospitals,
of which three-quarters tested positive for drugs at birth. Infants
hospitalized for extended periods may learn to walk there, with
hospital maintenance costs nearly $1,500 a day.[1]

The abandonment of children is not a recent historical phenomenon–it conjures images prevalent throughout Western history. In
literature, children often die by drowning, smothering, or being left
in a forest on the orders of a king. Medieval illustrations rarely
portray any human activity with children–women are not shown in
the mothering role. Occasionally, there are illustrations or stone
carvings with parents teaching a child to walk or cutting a child's
hair. Actually, as Firestone notes, during the Middle Ages there was
no such thing as childhood; the culture was not child-centered.
Children and adults were not distinct from one another. Children
depicted in medieval iconography are miniature adults, reflecting a
wholly different social reality.

Children then *were* tiny adults, carriers of whatever class and
name they had been born to, destined to rise into a clearly

outlined social position. A child saw himself as the future
adult going through his stages of apprenticeship; he was his
future powerful self 'when I was little.' He moved into the
various stages of his adult role almost immediately. . . . Children were so little differentiated from adults that there was no
special vocabulary to describe them: they shared the vocabulary of feudal subordination; only later, with the introduction
of childhood as a distinct state, is this confused vocabulary
separate.[2]

Owing to the high infant mortality rate of the times, estimated at
one or two in three, the investment of love in a young child was
unrewarding. Perhaps also the frequent childbearing put less value
on the product because a child was born and died and another took
its place.[3]

If children survived to age seven, their recognized life began,
more or less as miniature adults. Childhood was already over.
The immaturity observed in medieval behavior, with an inability to restrain impulses, was simply caused by a proportion of
active society young in years. About half the population, it has
been estimated, was under twenty-one, and about one third
under fourteen.[4]

Boswell points out that the concept of childhood is enigmatic,
and in his analysis of the abandonment of children, he states that
historical context oftentimes explains parental forfeiting of responsibility for a child rather than "simply forwarding a young person to
the ordinary next stage of life according to contemporary expectations." Actually, there was no concept of childhood in premodern
Europe: parent-child relations in previous ages were inherently and
categorically different from those in modern Western society.

The concept of child abuse is a contemporary phenomenon because almost all human societies have historically regarded children
as the property of their parents. This attitude was slightly modified
by law. As recently as the nineteenth century, children were without
human or civil rights that conflicted with parental wishes. In 1889,
Great Britain passed a national law aimed at preventing cruelty to
children in their homes at the urging of the National Society for the

Prevention of Cruelty to Children. Earlier statutes had outlawed the abandonment of infants by simply leaving them outdoors and the ill treatment of apprentices, youngsters living with and working free for merchants in order to learn a skill. A law of 1868 had made it a punishable offense for parents to neglect giving their children food, shelter, clothing, and medical care. In the United States, New York was the first state to pass, in 1875, a child protection law. The New York law served as a model for the other states, all of which now have laws making child abuse a criminal offense.

The number of special-needs cases has increased steadily over the past decade as the number of reported instances of physical and sexual abuse of children has risen. Judges are more willing to remove children from homes in which the parents are abusive. Nearly 60 percent of the foster-care caseload are abused children. With the HIV disease epidemic, as well, there is an increased caseload of HIV-infected infants and orphaned children. Substance use may be considered a dual epidemic with HIV disease. One estimate suggests that there are 365,000 American babies endangered by drugs *in utero,* two-thirds of whom were victims of crack/cocaine. Unlike other illicit drugs, crack/cocaine entices as many women as men, devastating family life. As new cases deluge the child welfare system, the number of foster parents has been declining, with more women working and hence unavailable to provide foster care. For special-needs children suffering the effects of mistreatment or prenatal drug use, the future may depend crucially on quickly finding a stable, nurturing home.

Special-needs children represent the majority of the population managed by the public adoption agencies of most states. Many couples seek healthy caucasian infants. Of the approximately 36,000 available special-needs babies, about one-third remain in hospitals—so-called *boarder babies* abandoned at birth by substance-using or otherwise incapable mothers.

Faced with the scarcity of couples for the growing numbers of special-needs children, adoption officials attempt to modify traditional conceptions of what constitutes a family. A White House task force recommended eliminating barriers to adoption by individuals such as working couples, older people, and the physically challenged. While the task force opposed adoption by lesbians and gay

men, growing numbers of such women and men, generally spurned
by ordinary adoption agencies, have adopted special-needs children.
Even when adoptive parents come forward, the foster-care and adoptive system often keep the children frustratingly out of reach. Designed to be a short-term arrangement ending in either adoption or
the child's return to a competent parent, foster care has become a
kind of sentence of indeterminate length. Approximately half of all
foster children return home, while many others are kept in legal
limbo by parents who make little effort to regain their children but
refuse to relinquish them fully. Federal law mandates that a mother
who shows no inclination to plan for a child within 18 months must
permit an adoption. However, absentee parents often obstruct attempts by making at least minimal contact during the 18 months. In
1986, the last year for calculated statistics, of an estimated 276,000
children in foster care, only 13 percent were immediately available
for adoption. In New York City, an adoption-counseling unit advises
drug-addicted birth mothers during hospitalization, explaining the
possibility of giving up parental rights and placing their child up for
adoption.

The exact incidence of child abuse and neglect in the United
States is unknown, but it is recognized as a major social problem.
Child abuse is the intentional use of physical force or intentional
omission of care by a parent or caretaker that causes a child to be
harmed, maimed, or killed. (See Figure 2.1 for the types of maltreatment.) Under state laws, several licensed professionals, such as
physicians and social workers, must report incidents of suspected
abuse. All states have laws requiring the reporting of suspected
cases of abuse. Typical social service responses to these reports
involve agency investigations and court proceedings to gain physical custody of a child deemed "in need of care and protection."
Sometimes, the child is separated from a parent and placed in a
foster home. The Federal Adoption Assistance and Child Welfare
Act of 1980 placed special emphasis on reducing the number of
children in foster care through an expansion of family-based services. Today, many states have established specific units within
their child welfare system to secure the therapeutic and support
services necessary to keep families together. More than 2 million
cases of neglect and physical abuse are reported annually, and of the

FIGURE 2.1. Child Abuse and Neglect Cases: Types of Maltreatment (Reported Cases = 918,263)

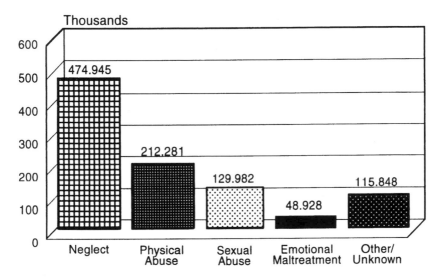

Source: U.S. Department of Health and Human Services, 1994.

estimated hundreds of thousands of children battered each year by a parent or close relative, thousands die. For those who survive, the emotional trauma remains long after the external bruises have healed. These emotional hidden bruises can be treated. Often the severe emotional damage to abused children does not surface until adolescence or later, when many abused children become abusing parents. Figure 2.2 outlines several symptoms, gathered from clinical practice, that manifest in abused children. Adults abused as children have difficulty establishing intimate personal relationships: they tend to see other adults as potential abusers. These individuals do not like to be touched, and, without treatment, they experience lifelong dysfunctionality. There are two ways of inflicting pain: one is an assault on the body, the other on the mind and emotions, and in every society children are victimized in both ways. Unfortunately, child abusers are most often the children's parents, though they are sometimes acquaintances or complete strangers.

FIGURE 2.2. Behavior of Sexually Abused Children

- Unusual interest or avoidance of all things of a sexual nature
- Sleep problems and nightmares
- Depression or withdrawal from friends or family
- Seductiveness
- Statements that their bodies are dirty or damaged
- Fear that something is wrong with them in the genital area
- Refusal to go to school
- Delinquency
- Secretiveness
- Aspects of sexual molestation in drawings, games, fantasies
- Unusual aggressiveness
- Suicidal behavior
- Poor self-image
- Inability to depend on or trust others
- Aggressive or disruptive, sometimes illegal, behavior
- Passive and withdrawn behavior
- Drug and alcohol use

The forms of abuse that inflict pain upon the body include beating, burning, stabbing, shooting, and sexual abuse. The latter has become frighteningly common. In addition, tens of thousands of children are kidnapped every year, many of whom are forced into prostitution and the making of pornographic movies.

Nonphysical abuse may be obvious, such as constantly screaming accusations of blame, or snide, undeserved criticisms or put-downs. It may also be far less apparent but no less real. Emotionally neglected children, even though they may be taken care of materially, suffer this form of child abuse or indifference. Such abuse is not benign neglect, but derives from parents not very interested in their children. Such parents nearly always deny their indifference to everybody, including themselves.

Even though there are numerous studies of child abuse, it is not easy to determine its causes. It is not limited to one social class, though there seems to be a higher incidence of physical child abuse among the very poor. Quite often children are victimized by parents who find themselves suddenly unemployed. Such abuse is more likely to be the result of the parent's anger and frustration with his or her status than of any real hostility toward the child. The results of child abuse are as detrimental as the cruelty itself. If the children survive, and many do not, they find themselves either physically neglected or emotionally harmed, or both. In poor families, an abused child frequently suffers from lack of feeding and absence of medical care, and education is neglected or parents are indifferent. Physical neglect can do damage to the brain and other parts of the body from which the individual may never recover.

The emotional scars from child abuse are deep and require treatment to heal. Abused children feel that there is something wrong with them or they would not be mistreated. As they continue to blame themselves for their fate, their self-esteem declines to the point that they despise themselves and everyone else as well. Adolescents often do not blame their parents or relatives for what they have suffered but instead turn on society and become delinquents, troublemakers at school, runaways, or criminals. When courts or social agencies remove abused children from their parents' home and place them in a healthy home environment, then long-term damage can be minimized.

Child abuse covers a wide range of parental actions that result in harm being inflicted on children of all ages. The kind of abuse, however, varies with age. Infants and preschool children are more likely to suffer deliberately inflicted fractures, burns, and bruises. This is termed *battered-child syndrome*. Historically, reported cases of sexual abuse, ranging from molestation to incest, primarily involved male perpetrators and school-age or adolescent female victims. Recently, a growing number of preschool victims and male victims have been identified. Some states have broadened their statutory definitions of abuse to specifically include emotional or mental injury. Constant parental rejection, for example, can permanently cripple a child's personality.

Perhaps the most prevalent type of abuse is neglect—that is, physical or emotional harm resulting from a parent's failure to provide a child with adequate food, clothing, shelter, medical care, education, and moral training. A common symptom of neglect among young children is underfeeding; an undernourished infant often fails to thrive and may even die. In the age range between 8 and 17 years, neglect, as opposed to physical or sexual abuse, was involved in about 70 percent of all validated reports of mistreatment in the United States. See Figure 2.3 for ages of abused children.

Studies have shown that most child-abusing parents were themselves abused children. Some researchers assert that abusing parents have infantile personalities. Others note that abusing parents unrealistically expect their children to fulfill their psychological needs; when disappointed, the parent experiences severe stress and becomes violently angry and abusive. In spite of this emphasis on individual psychopathology, few child abusers are diagnosed as psychotic or sociopathological. Incidents of abuse occur among all religious, eth-

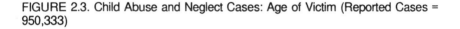

FIGURE 2.3. Child Abuse and Neglect Cases: Age of Victim (Reported Cases = 950,333)

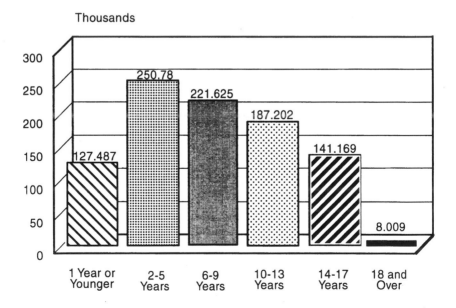

Source: U.S. Department of Health and Human Services, 1994.

nic, and racial groups and in all geographic areas. The relationship between poverty and abuse is strong; the vast majority of fatalities involve parents and caretakers from the poorest families.

In the United States, public concern about the growing incidence of child abuse has led to the enactment of both state and federal legislation. Although the focus remains on identifying, reporting, and treating cases of abuse, prevention efforts are increasing. Since 1980, some 45 states have established specific resources for child abuse prevention services. Under the 1962 amendments to the 1935 Social Security Act, state public welfare agencies are responsible for child protection. Because effective solutions cannot be achieved without clear data about the dimensions of a problem, the 1974 Federal Child Abuse Prevention and Treatment Act was an important legislative measure. It mandated establishment of a major program of research, demonstration, training, dissemination of information, and financial grants to the states by a National Center on Child Abuse and Neglect.

Projects that provide short-term relief from child-rearing situations and a range of concrete supportive services to parents have demonstrated that child abuse often occurs when parents are under severe and unremitting stress as a result of events within the family environment over which they have no control. To avert a significant percentage of separation of families and to solve the problem of child abuse, the major role that social and economic forces play must be better understood. Effective prevention requires a fundamental change in societal values and public priorities in order to correct the conditions of poverty, unemployment, inadequate housing, and ill health, which are found in the overwhelming majority of abusing families. It is also necessary to place a greater emphasis on the rights of children and the responsibilities of parents toward their children.

Child sexual abuse has been reported up to 80,000 times a year, but the number of unreported incidents, though undoubtedly high, cannot be known for certain because the children are afraid to tell anyone what has happened, and the legal procedure for validating an episode is difficult. The problem should be identified, the abuse stopped, and the child should receive professional help. The long-term emotional and psychological damage can be devastating.

Child sexual abuse can take place within the family, by a parent, stepparent, sibling, or other relative; or outside the home, by a friend, neighbor, child care provider, teacher, or random molester. However, in whatever environment the sexual abuse has occurred, the child develops a variety of distressing feelings and thoughts. No child is psychologically prepared to cope with repeated sexual stimulation. Even a two- or three-year-old, who cannot know the sexual activity is "wrong," will develop problems resulting from the inability to cope with the overstimulation.

The child of five or older who knows and cares for the abuser becomes trapped between affection or loyalty for the person and the sense that the sexual activities are terribly wrong. If the child tries to break away from the sexual relationship, the abuser may threaten the child with violence or loss of love. When sexual abuse occurs within the family, the child may fear the anger, jealousy, or shame of other family members, or he or she may be afraid the family will break up if the secret is told.

A child who is the victim of prolonged sexual abuse usually develops low self-esteem, a feeling of worthlessness, and an abnormal perspective on sexuality. The child may become withdrawn and mistrustful of adults, and can become suicidal. Some children who have been sexually abused have difficulty relating to others except on sexual terms. Some sexually abused children become child abusers or prostitutes, or have other serious problems when they reach adulthood. Often there are no physical signs of child abuse, or there are signs that only a physician can detect, such as changes in the genital or anal area. Child sexual abusers can make the child extremely fearful of telling, and only when a special effort has helped the child to feel safe can the child talk freely. If a child says that he or she has been molested, parents should stress that what happened was not the fault of the child. Parents should seek a medical examination and psychiatric consultation.

These are some preventive measures that parents can take. Tell children that "if someone tries to touch your body and do things that make you feel funny, say NO to that person and tell me right away." Teach children that respect does not mean blind obedience to adults and to authority—for example, don't tell children to "always do everything the teacher or baby-sitter tells you to do." Encourage professional prevention programs in the local school system.

Professional evaluation and treatment as soon as possible for the sexually abused child and the family is the best way to overcome the risk that the child will develop serious problems as an adult. The child and adolescent psychiatrist helps the child regain a sense of self-esteem and relieve feelings of guilt about the abuse; helps family members understand how to assist the child in overcoming the trauma; and, if the abuser is a member of the family, works to restore him or her to a healthy role in the family.

Investigative journalists have reported scandalous undetected evidence of infanticide in many regions of the United States. Without an autopsy, it is almost impossible to detect a child-abuse murder, and other siblings are in jeopardy when a murder is undetected. One investigation revealed that children are sometimes buried without a known cause of death identified by medical examiners or coroners, who have deferred to parental wishes not to perform an autopsy to determine the cause of a child's death. Almost 5,000 seemingly healthy babies die inexplicably each year.[5]

> Three children die of abuse every day, but at least three more a day are thought to go undetected because these children are not autopsied although pathology findings are crucial to detecting child abuse. Of the 7,422 most suspicious child deaths in the United States, 531 were not autopsied. Almost one in 12 child deaths blamed on Sudden Infant Death Syndrome (SIDS) were not autopsied, which is a violation of accepted medical procedure. In 1989, a record 1,237 children died from abuse, a rise of 39% in four years, says the National Committee for Prevention of Child Abuse. Authorities are convinced many more were murdered.[6]

Lack of money stops some death investigations because autopsies take two to four hours and cost about $950. No infant death should be called SIDS without an autopsy, the National Institutes of Health says, because SIDS itself is a medical mystery—a sudden death that remains inexplicable even after autopsy.

Children who are driven to kill abusive parents, statistics suggest, are from 16 to 18 years old, come from white middle-class families, and have above-average intelligence, although their schoolwork may be below average. They generally are well-adjusted in school and the community, though they tend to be isolated, without many friends. They commonly have had no prior run-in with the law. Their target is most often the father—usually a biological parent or stepparent rather than an adoptive or foster parent—and the typical weapon is a gun kept in the home.

> Today youngsters who slay abusive parents are drawing more understanding from a public that has awakened to the national nightmare of child abuse. Last year an estimated 2.7 million youngsters were physically, mentally and sexually assaulted by their parents, according to the National Center for Prevention of Child Abuse. Despite the prevalence of abuse, parricide remains rare. It accounts for about 2% of all homicides, around 300 cases a year. Most of those involve teenagers who kill abusive parents.[7]

These young people generally do not show any obvious signs of the mental disorders and self-destructive tendencies shared by children who strike out at strangers on the street or at nonabusive parents.

Children are also victims of kidnapping, with the majority of the several hundred thousand incidents a year perpetrated by family members in custody disputes. In 1990, in its report, *National Incidence Studies on Missing, Abducted and Thrown-Away Children* in America, the United States Justice Department stated that far fewer children—3,200 to 4,600 minors a year—are seized by strangers. Most victims are teenagers and a disproportionate number are African American or Hispanic. Only 300 of the abductions are classic kidnappings involving overnight captivity, transport of more than 50 miles, and ransom or murder. The number of kidnap-murders has fluctuated between 50 and 150 a year for at least 17 years.[8]

Indentured slavery of children into prostitution is a global problem from Thailand and India to Latin America and the United States. Sexual tourism is uncontrolled with centers of child prostitution in every country. Sexual tourists usually do not use condoms, exposing children to the risk of AIDS, and seek out ever younger victims in the belief they will be free from sexual diseases.

It is believed some 200,000 Nepali girls have been sold into sexual slavery in Indian brothels. It is a serious problem in Brazil. Probably 60,000 children work as prostitutes in the Philippine sex industry, and perhaps as many as 200,000 in Thailand. In Colombia, for example, it said the number of child prostitutes in the capital has risen fivefold in seven years. A third of all prostitutes are under 14 and one in 20 is under 10. Some nations specialise in boy prostitutes. . . . In Moscow alone an estimated 1,000 boys and girls of tender age are selling their bodies. Three years ago, police say, there were only a very few. A similar rise in child prostitution has occurred in other Russian and East European cities. In the Third World the numbers are also staggering: an estimated 800,000 underage prostitutes in Thailand, 400,000 in India, 250,000 in Brazil and 60,000 in the Philippines. The newest international sites for child prostitution: Vietnam, Cambodia, Laos, China and the Dominican Republic.[9]

It is essential to engage as rapidly and forcefully as possible in efforts that reduce the risk of HIV infection to prostitutes and the possibility of transmission to others. To facilitate this there is a need for uniform evaluation techniques for sociodemographic, psychosocial, biomedical, and clinical data on prostitution and HIV transmission.

Child prostitution is no less a product of poverty and drugs in the United States than it is in underdeveloped countries. Estimates of the number of U.S. prostitutes under age 18 range from 90,000 to 300,000. Poor teenagers sell their bodies to acquire drugs, jewelry, or even food and household items for their families. The sex trade among children receives a further boost in the United States and elsewhere by the child pornography industry. In Germany, annual sales of "kiddie porn" are estimated at $250 million, and the number of consumers is estimated at between 30,000 and 40,000. Since penalties in developed countries are severe, most dealers buy films made in Asia, where operations can be easily run from hotel rooms and where there is an abundance of potential victims in the streets.

One of the more tragic, and ironic, reasons for the recent upswing in child prostitution is the mistaken belief that young sex partners are less likely to have AIDS. In fact, the opposite may be true. One survey found that more than 50 percent of Thai child prostitutes are HIV positive.

> "The sex industry is a huge market with its own momentum," says Wassyla Tamzali, director of UNESCO's women's-rights department. "You have an internal race between the client and the pimp to expand the boundaries, to find the newest experience possible. Selling a 14-year-old girl has become so commonplace, it is banal."[10]

A 1991 conference of Southeast Asian women's organizations estimated that 30 million women had been sold worldwide since the mid-1970s. Globally, prostitution plays a significant role in transmitting the AIDS virus.

In 1989, the General Assembly of the United Nations summoned the Convention on the Rights of the Child to protect the integrity of children from any "arbitrary or unlawful interference with his or her privacy, family, home or correspondence, [or] unlawful attacks on his or her honour and reputation."[11] They proposed measures to include effective procedures for the "establishment of social programs to provide support for the child and for those who have the care of the child, as well as for other forms of prevention and for identification, reporting, referral, investigation, treatment, and follow-up of instances of child maltreatment to protect children from all forms of physical or mental violence, injury or abuse, neglect or negligent treatment, maltreatment or exploitation, including sexual abuse, while in the care of parents, legal guardians, or any other person who has the care of the child." The National Child Rights Alliance believes that civil rights apply to all people, including children and youth:

> No children shall be forced to live in any household against their will–this includes biologic as well as foster and adoptive households. No children shall be forced into marriage. No children shall be institutionalized against their will without due process rights. . . . No child shall be either forced or forbidden to choose a religious or political affiliation, philosophy or creed.[12]

In its Youth Bill of Rights, the National Child Rights Alliance declared children's rights to liberty; safety; survival; education; free speech; nondiscrimination on the basis of age, race, gender, language, country of origin, economic or marital status of parents, religious or sexual preference, and physical or mental limitations or differences; free choice; and the right to an attorney.

NOTES

1. D. Van Biema, Mother and Child Reunion. *Time* January 24, 1994.

2. S. Firestone *The Dialectic of Sex* (New York: Bantam, 1971), 76-77.

3. B. Tuchman *A Distant Mirror* (New York: Knopf, 1978), 49-50.

4. Ibid, 52.

5. R. Sharpe and M. Lundstrom, Failure to Investigate Suspicious Deaths of Children is Criminal. *USA Today* April 11, 1991.

6. M. Lundstrom and R. Sharpe, It's Easy to Kill a Child. *USA Today* December 17, 1990.

7. A. Toufexis, When Kids Kill Abusive Parents. *Time* November 23, 1992.

8. D. Van Biema, Robbing the Innocents. *Time* December 29, 1993.

9. M.S. Serrill, Defiling the Children. *Time* June 21, 1993.

10. *Op cit.*

11. United Nations, The General Assembly, Convention on the Rights of the Child, November 1989.

12. Youth Bill of Rights, National Child Rights Alliance, September 1989.

Chapter 3

To Everything There Is a Season

Children's liberation is the next item on our civil rights shopping list.

Letty Cottin Pogrebin,
"Down with Sexist Upbringing,"
in *The First Ms. Reader*,
ed. by Francine Klagsbrun

They live on a street opposite Central Park in a row of brownstones converted into apartment buildings. Renee is the adoptive mother of a ten-year-old daughter, Toni, whose mother died of HIV disease five years ago. Renee is a single mother who is a practicing social worker for an agency that provides services for so-called at-risk adolescents. Renee adopted her daughter a year after being her foster mother.

Above the round oak table where the three of us sat was a large reproduction of the Degas pastel *After the Bath, Woman Drying Herself*. Pastels are popular for artists because they take less time than painting in oil. For Toni, there was only time, time to heal, as in the book of Ecclesiastes. Toni was five years old when her mother, Teresa, known as Terry, died of HIV disease, and despite her young age, she has vivid memories of her. Renee was attending graduate school at New York University, getting her master's degree in social work, when she first met Terry and Toni as a case manager at the New York City's Human Resource Administration (HRA), Division of AIDS Services (DAS). DAS was created to manage the caseloads of persons with AIDS during the 1980s, and a major function of the unit is to place homeless individuals.

Renee remembers, "Terry was one of the most difficult clients I had. I guess it was mostly because she was so verbally abusive. She didn't trust anyone, wore it like a badge. She was very smart. Well, I should say street-smart. A little paranoid, the kind of paranoia one earns in order to survive in the world of poverty and systems combined with drug-induced paranoia."

When Terry became a DAS client, her sister Maria was critically ill at Montefiore Hospital in the Bronx with her second bout of pneumocystis cariini pneumonia (PCP)—she was on a respirator. Maria had two children, Yolanda and James. They had been placed in foster care because of Maria's active substance use. Each child had a different guardian. Maria and Terry shared everything—men, misery, needles—and probably had become reinfected, cross-infected with HIV many times over the years. Renee remembered Terry saying, "I'm next. I'm going to follow my sister to the grave." It turned out to be prophetic because they died within of week of each other. But Terry's death was from a suicidal drug overdose. Renee stated, "I knew that I wanted to take care of Toni, become her foster mother. It was almost reflexive for me. Everyone at the agency was opposed to it, from my supervisor to my colleagues, but I was resolute. At first, I became a foster mother, but within the year I decided to adopt Toni."

Our discussion was punctuated by the cracking rhythm of claves, as Toni struck the percussion sticks used widely in Latin American music. She held one stick between her thumb and forefinger, striking the second stick, which rested across the small cupped palm of her other hand. She ritualistically accompanied the rumba dance music playing on her portable stereo, sounding an unchanging background rhythm.

Renee recalled, "I don't think that Terry knew who was Toni's father. She was turning tricks for drugs, and I didn't believe she protected herself from HIV or pregnancy. When Toni was three years old she was placed in foster care by the child welfare agency because Terry was unable to take care of her. Terry was doing sex work somewhere in the Bronx, sleeping on rooftops in the summer and in hallways when the weather was cold. She looked awful when I first met her after her first hospitalization with PCP and must've known that she had HIV infection, barely able to climb a flight of stairs." Renee became anxious, fingering an unlit cigarette, becoming distracted by a screen memory, perhaps a memory of something unconscious, a recollection of an associated but distressing event.

"I remember the first time I saw her. I was having a terrible day, and the night before Jeff and I had a huge fight. Jeff was the man I was seeing at the time. I spent half the relationship trying to diagnose him and the other half trying to get him into treatment. The last thing I needed that day was Terry. Every word out of her mouth was fuck this and fuck that, and when it became fuck you, it was more than I could take, especially after I was describing the services we would provide for her, most importantly a furnished apartment. She said agitatedly, 'I don't want The Bronx, or Brooklyn. Or some rat-infested SRO crack den.' She paused for a moment during her diatribe to ask, 'Can you help me get my daughter back? I want my daughter.' At that moment, I felt her pain, experienced her humanity. I said I would help.

"We worked together for about six months. Terry moved into an apartment on the upper West Side, she stayed clean, stopped the sex work, and accepted her new life clean. She was able to get Toni back, but it wasn't easy for her because her health continued to deteriorate. She began to become demented, only slightly at first, mere forgetfulness. Then after a few months, it worsened with dizzy spells, falling, and spatial problems. She cut her forehead walking into a wall and required four stitches. Home care became a necessity, which was very difficult for her."

Renee remembered deciding to have Toni HIV tested. "Toni had not been antibody tested for HIV, and while her health appeared stable, there have been incidences where symptomatology does not manifest until prepuberty. I decided to have her tested by a physician I knew well whose work was with pediatric HIV cases. Waiting for the result was excruciating, and when the result came back negative, I just wept."

We arranged for me to spend time with Toni alone and decided on an activity away from the apartment. Toni and I walked toward Central Park, deciding to go to the zoo. She seemed surprisingly unguarded, holding my hand as we crossed the street to the park entrance. I asked her as we walked through Strawberry Fields, the section of the park dedicated to John Lennon, "If you just met someone for the first time . . ."

She interrupted, "Like you?"

"Yes. And you wanted to tell them something about yourself. Tell me what you'd say."

She hesitated at first, then said, "Well. First, I'd try to get to know them a little bit. Like my new school. I had to get to know them and get used to them being around me. And, maybe if I learned to trust them, then I could start to tell them stuff about me."

"What would you like to tell them?"

"Well, that my parents died. That my parents did drugs. They weren't very . . . well . . ." She paused, not wanting to reveal her feelings, then continued. "They had AIDS. Actually, I never met my father. I would tell them I'm adopted. I was adopted by a lady named Renee, and this family is much better than the last one."

I questioned, "How is this family different?"

"Well, because they don't . . . Let's say you didn't want to do something, you would have to do something. I was always afraid. When I first moved here, it was like, I wouldn't do anything because I was too scared to. And because when I was living there I would get into trouble if I did. So I always acted like Miss Perfect."

She looked away and seemed not to want to pursue discussion of her mother, but I continued by asking, "Can you remember way back when you were little?"

"I can sorta. Well, I think as far back as I can remember was when my mom first died and I went to her funeral. And I was about four then, I think. I think my sister knows. And when my mom died I was really, really sad. I kept sobbing and sobbing every night and I couldn't fall asleep. Because she was like the only real nice person to me besides my cousin and sister. My aunt always made me do stuff that was really uncomfortable doing. Like sometimes she would . . . And I was so scared when she yelled at me."

"What would she make you do?"

"I thought that I was like her maid because I was doing everything for her. And I didn't like that. I was only a little girl. She didn't know how to take care of herself. She was a little crazy. And my sister is now living with someone who is definitely crazy too and she can't even take care of herself. She still lives with her parents. She has two babies and she can't take care of them. One time we went over there . . . um . . . She was making faces at my mom."

"What is the first thing you can remember? Not something that someone told you."

"The first thing I can remember . . . After my mom died my sister took me to Central Park. I think we went to the zoo or something, maybe ice skating. Well, I'm not sure if that was before my mom died. And we got lost. I think that's it."

"What makes a mother good? What does she have to do? Not your mother, but any mother."

"She has to remember to do stuff for her child. Not forget her children in school. I don't think she should do drugs or drink, and if she did do that before she had a child, she should go to meetings."

"What do you mean by meetings?"

"A place you go to talk about your feelings. How you get all those bad feelings out, and so you don't keeping them all building up inside. So you don't dump them on your child when it's not their fault."

"What does a father have to do to be a good father?"

"I never met my father. He shouldn't drink. I forgot to say something about the mother or the father. They shouldn't beat their children. Because then their children will grow up to be, any child, will grow up to be, and if they have children, they'll be like their parents. They'll learn from their parents and think that's right."

"Did you ever see that happen?"

"Well. Yeah. When I went to my old school, there's a boy there named Ralph and he's the bully of the school. Like he'd tease me ten times a day. My cousin went to camp with him, and he was a counselor. And he said he lies a lot because that summer he said he was moving down south and he wasn't going back to P.S. 299. And he didn't move down south. I think that his parents are like that at home. He always got into fights. He started hitting people. So I think his parents are setting a bad example."

I said to her, "I'm going to tell you a story and you'll finish it. Let's pretend there was a baby bird, living in a nest with a mother bird and a father bird. The baby bird could fly just a little bit. Then along came a big wind that blew the mother bird out of the nest one way and blew the father bird out another way. Let's make up a story about what happened to the baby bird. Remember the baby bird could just fly a little bit."

"Well, it would try to get to the ground. I think it would have fallen down. I would hope that it would be able to stop. Like, it would stop with its feet. It would have its wings out to the side for protection. Did he know how to get his own food? He knew that worms were under the ground. He started digging with his beak. Could you make it like the father and mother came back? And so a few days went by. He ate worms and he built . . . He found a bush. And like he slept in the bushes. And after a week passed, his parents came looking for him. And they went back. The mother made him a nest where he was sleeping."

"It that the end of the story?"

"The end."

"You and I know that sometimes children are afraid of things. Like before they go to kindergarten or the first grade."

"Or a new school."

"Yes. They're afraid of the dark or storms or ghosts or robbers or kidnappers. Tell me what you were afraid of when you were little."

"I think I was mostly afraid of . . . My sister sometimes used to tease me that the boogie man was coming to get me. And I didn't like that and was scared of him. I was scared of ghosts on my own. Like on Halloween I wouldn't go trick or treating cause . . . Well, first of all I didn't have a costume and second of all I was scared. And I think I was scared of kidnappers because I didn't want to get taken away from my family. Plus I'd be separated from my sister. I wouldn't even be able to go into a foster home. Third of all, I wouldn't even be here. So, I didn't want to be kidnapped. Once I was. When I was a little, little baby. I was. My sister told me that a man had tooken me. And she was like, 'Please mister. Please mister. Give me back my little sister. Or else my mom will spank me.' So the father came along. My sister's father came along. We both have different fathers. I think it was him or even our mother. He was behind him and punched him. I don't know what he did, but he got me back. I think this was my mother. So . . . Then we got home and somebody said . . . Oh no. I think my sister went home. She told her father. Then she said, 'Oh no. No. No. Daddy, I'm sorry I didn't get the baby.' Then my mother walked in and she had me in her arms. So I could've got kidnapped. I was only three then."

"Tell me about going to the new school."

"First that was just in September. I was going to a new school, and I really didn't want to go the first day. Because at my old school when I first got a short haircut, they were sitting there and teased me. I didn't like being teased.

"In my new school, my mom and the bus didn't come that day. And we had to take a cab, and we were waiting and waiting. I said, 'Can we just go home because the bus isn't coming?' 'No. We're going in the cab if the bus doesn't come in five minutes.' And when we were in the cab, I went, 'Mommy, do I have to go to school?' I really didn't want to go to school. But it wasn't so bad."

"Tell me how they teased you about the haircut."

"It was mostly Ralph. He kept saying, 'Look at that boy.'"

"You and I know that everybody has dreams."

"Yeah."

"Good ones and bad ones. Tell me a dream you remember."

"A good one *or* bad one?"

"Yes."

"Well . . . Well, it's a scary dream. It includes me, my cousin, and my sister. This dream always frightened me. We were in this cottage deep in the woods, and there was nobody there. We were just like . . . I think my sister was cooking. Chicken and rice. She's a really good cook. Or maybe it was rice and beans. Me and my cousin . . . I think he was telling me a story. All of a sudden when we were looking at the window along came this man. He came inside the cottage. Then I woke up."

"Did you have the dream more than once?"

"No. Only once. I also had a good dream. It's kind of funny. I was a teenage girl, practicing for the Olympics. Like, tryouts. Olympics gymnastics. And there I am at night in France. All of a sudden, I'm the first . . . Um. I have a gold medal on. On my neck for bars. It's really funny."

"You mentioned before that you're adopted."

"Yeah."

"Tell me what you think about that?"

"Well, my mom says that it's a special thing. Not many people are allowed to go through a foster agency and pick out who they want to be their child. It doesn't happen that you choose your child when you get pregnant–you don't know what your child is going to look like. And you're kind of stuck with it. My mom said she was lucky because she got to pick me out. But I was never in a foster home, I just went to her work. My mother and my aunt went to her, she was their helper, and they sometimes brought me with them. One day they weren't there, and I'm not sure what happened. They weren't there one day, and I think that's what happened."

"Do you know any other children who are adopted?"

"Yeah. A girl in my gymnastics class. She's kind of braggy. She's very flexible, but can't do gymnastics. She lies a lot. She says I was adopted with her, but I wasn't."

"Why do you think she says that?"

"To make me feel better, but that doesn't make me feel better because it's a big lie. I wasn't adopted with her at all. I just met her this summer."

"Tell me why she'd want you to feel better."

"I don't know–that's what I'm guessing because I think she'd just like to do it."

"What do you remember about your mother?"

"She looked mostly like me. She had blue eyes, a pointy nose, and I don't remember what her lips looked like. She had long hair and was pale-ish."

"You said that you had gone to her funeral and you cried a lot."

"Yeah."

"Tell me what you know about death, when someone dies."

"That they lived their life, but she was young. When they're ready to die . . . but she wasn't necessarily ready. She had the AIDS. She did drugs and drank alcohol. She was ready to die, and it wasn't old age, but she was ready to die. So I don't really blame her because she was really sick then and a little bit crazy."

"What do you think happens when someone dies?"

"You go to heaven and become an angel. But, a lot of kids told me if you were bad and killed somebody, then you would go to hell where the devil was. And if you did something good in your life, and really lived a good life then you would go to heaven and become an angel."

"Tell me what you know about angels?"

"It's really cool to be an angel. I think God . . . I think there are two gods. The good god is the head of the angels. And the bad god is the devil of devils who rules down underground."

"What does an angel look like?"

"I think it's like cupid. The head angel . . . all the little angels look like cupid, and the head angel is the mightiest of the mightiest and the oldest and wisest. The head angel knows a lot. The head angel is kind of old, but stays alive forever."

"When someone dies do you ever see them again?"

"No I don't think. But, I think they see you and watch over you. I think if you go to their grave, you can actually see them. They look just the same as they did, but not so sick if they were sick, not so old if they were old. They look like they did when they were really young and healthy. But I haven't been to a graveyard in a very long time."

"You mentioned AIDS. What do you know about AIDS?"

"I know that you can catch it a certain way about sharing needles, having unsafe sex. You can't catch it by hugging someone. Or holding hands or going to the same camp with them. They're people like you and me. They don't want to be treated differently. You shouldn't treat them differently. If you want to protect yourself from AIDS, I think wear a condom and don't share needles."

"You know so much about AIDS."

"Well, I watched this thing on TV when Magic Johnson got AIDS, 'A Talk with Magic,' and they talked all about wearing a condom and not sharing needles. So I know something about it, and my mom's told me. I had some questions."

"What questions did you have?"

"Well, why is there such a thing as AIDS? When I was really little, I asked her how to protect herself from AIDS. She talked a great deal about that."

"What did you learn?"

"When my mom was little, we didn't know anything about AIDS because they said it was a big lie. They said there's no such thing as AIDS. That's what my mom told me."

"Do you like Magic Johnson?"

"I'm not really into basketball, but I thought he was a neat basketball player. I think on the show he has a lot of really good things to say."

"Have you ever known anyone who was HIV positive?"

"I do know somebody, a grownup, but I don't think they'd want me to say their name. A friend of my mom and me. I think it would be kind of embarrassing to say his name."

"You were saying about being adopted. Do you miss having a father?"

"I don't really have a father. Sometimes I miss having a father and sometimes I don't. Sometime I like being with me and my mom alone. I'm not really used to having another person in the house. My mom has a friend named Ron, and he sometimes comes over. He's my mom's boyfriend but not really. Sometimes they have their fights. I think they're really not that close. Like boyfriend and girlfriend.

"I wasn't really used to having a man around. But he was giving me attention, so now I feel kind of okay about it. But, sometimes I want it to be just me and my mom. That's how I feel about it."

"Were the questions that I've been asking you hard?"

"No. It's kind of interesting that me and my sister are being interviewed. I don't know. It's kind of weird you could bring a family together and have an interview on this subject. It's weird. It probably doesn't happen that often. It's not usual to have a family whose parents had HIV, and all be related and interviewed on the subject. That's what's weird about it."

Signs are small measurable things, but interpretations are illimitable, and every sign in Toni's sweet nature conjured wonder, hope, and the belief, vast as the sky, that her life would be fine. We proceeded through the park by loops and zigzags. We remained in the zoo longer than intended, delighting in the camaraderie of polar bears. She spoke without fear of discomfort, for in looking backward through sadness she found solace. She remarked, "I thought that I'd like to talk to you again. It seems strange to me how many things I said to you." She was no longer struggling against the perception of facts, but adjusting herself to their clearest perception. We parted in front of her building and she leapt into my arms, planting a kiss on my cheek.

Chapter 4

Devices for Safekeeping

From the point of view of the pharmaceutical industry, the AIDS problem has already been solved. After all, we already have a drug which can be sold at the incredible price of $8,000 an annual dose, and which has the added virtue of not diminishing the market by actually curing anyone.

Barbara Ehrenreich,
"Phallic Science,"
The Worst Years of Our Lives, (1991)

In the early part of this century, social worker Etta Angel Wheeler discovered a nine-year-old girl wandering naked through the streets of a New York City slum after being beaten, slashed, and thrown out by her alcoholic foster mother. Wheeler appealed to the American Society for the Prevention of Cruelty to Animals (ASPCA) for lack of any other agency concerned with the well-being of children. The ASPCA decided the girl was an *animal* deserving of shelter, and prosecuted the foster mother for starving and abusing the child. The American Society for the Prevention of Cruelty to Children (ASPCC) was then created.

The community center is located on the periphery of Soho, which was once New York's avant-garde artists' neighborhood until the late 1960s, when living in factory lofts became fashionable and rents became prohibitively expensive. Now the streets of Soho are lined with trendy shops. It's several days after Christmas, and the center is preparing to observe *Kwanza*, an African-American, secular, seven-day festival, beginning on December 26. Kwanza is a prototype of traditional African harvest festivals. The holiday emphasizes the role of the family and community in African-American

culture. Each day celebrates a particular principle (unity, self-determination, collective work and responsibility, cooperative econom-
ics, purpose, creativity, and faith), and on each day one of the
candles on a seven-branched candelabrum is lighted. The celebra-
tion also includes the giving of gifts and a *karamu*, or African feast.

Raquel, 14 years old, has been in three foster homes since her
mother died five years ago. Quite unlike her sister, Lela, she is
unmistakably Latina, with mocha-colored skin and peroxide-high-
lighted brunette hair worn to her shoulders. She is overweight, a
fact that is noticable despite her baggy clothing: denim overalls
with a flannel shirt tied at the waist. She resisted being interviewed,
not wanting to experience vulnerability and relive painful past
events, but once Lela agreed, she felt it would be safe.

We met in the community center that services adolescents, many
of whom need long-term psychotherapy after crisis intervention
resolves the immediate problem. I arranged with her counselor to
meet Raquel in the group room. She was huddled in a corner,
wearing her coat and a knitted cap pulled to her eyebrows. She
greeted me succinctly with: "I'm cold."

"You're going to wrap yourself up? Tell me how old you are."

"I'm gonna be fifteen on December 20."

"What are your hobbies, what do you like doing?"

"Nothing. Ya know, if I don't know you, I don't want you to
know nothing."

"If you felt trusting, what would you say?"

"My habits. Hangin' out. Goin' round with your friends, stayin'
on the corner."

"Sometimes people can remember when they're very young; tell
me how far back you can remember."

"When I was two. My mother lost me. We was outside, and she
was paying attention to her friends. I was with my cousin and
walked away. She was lookin' for me, and they found me around
the corner. This man found me, and asked, 'Who you be?' Then my
mother found me. I got into trouble when my mother found me. I
remember that."

"You got into trouble?"

"Yeah, I walked away from my mother. She didn't take me, what
. . . She didn't take me outside for a year. I was sittin' at home, and

I didn't go to places where I had to like the store, no play, or nuttin'. I was always in the house."

"You were in the house for a year?"

"Not in the house . . . in the house, but I wasn't allowed to go outside or play with my cousin or anything. It was like an old, old person."

"Tell me what a mother has to do to be a good mother."

"I don't know. Take care of you. Feed you. Buy you clothes. That's it. I don't know. And the father, the same thing."

"How would you know if your parents love you?"

"By their takin' care of you and not leaving you. Or not beatin' you and stuff like that because I never got hit. That's why I'm bad. I ain't never got hit. I never had discipline with my mother."

"Tell me why you think you're bad."

"I don't go to school or do anything. I didn't like school. I don't like gettin' up in the morning. I just slept. But then things changed and I had to go to school and everything."

"I'm going to tell you a story and you'll finish it. Let's pretend there was a baby bird, living in a nest with a mother bird and a father bird. The baby bird could fly just a little bit. Then along came a big wind that blew the mother bird out of the nest one way and blew the father bird out another way. Let's make up a story about what happened to the baby bird. Remember the baby bird could just fly a little bit."

"It landed, and when it grew up it knew how to take care of itself. That's about it. It learned to take care of itself."

"What did it need to learn to take care of itself?"

"How to find food. I don't know. Where to live. How to fly."

"What happened to the bird when it got older?"

"I guess it took care of itself."

"You and I know that sometimes children are afraid of things. They're afraid of the dark or storms or ghosts or robbers or kidnappers. Tell me what you were afraid of when you were little."

"Waterbugs. The way they looked. I'm still scared of them til this day."

"What about now?"

"Not really. I know that's not good. But not really. You're supposed to have some kind of fear. But I don't. It ain't natural. You're supposed to have some kind of fear. Maybe when I get older I'll feel things, but not now."

"You and I know that everybody has dreams. Good ones and bad ones. Tell me a dream you remember."

"I lost my sister once. We was in a store, and I was sittin' on the stoop. And they wouldn't let me get my sister. And I was screamin' her name, but she wouldn't come outside. I looked for her when I woke up. She was in the bed with my grandmother."

"Tell me what happened to your mother?"

"She died."

"Do you think about her?"

"Of course. I miss her. She's gone. She's in another place. A different world. I don't know what it looks like. Just white. Just white clouds and stuff."

"How old were you when your mother died?"

"I don't remember. I don't remember nuttin' really. But I remember everything. I used to have dreams about her, but not recently. I dreamt she came back alive. She was dead, I remember her being dead in the dream. She was like a nun or something. If she got cut, she would die. She got cut or something on the bottom of her foot. She had died again, I dunno. It was a dream like that. I don't think death looks like anything."

"Tell me what you know about AIDS."

"It's a disease. I know how you catch it, by sex or intravenous drugs, stuff like that. You can't get it by hugging or kissing, or drinking out of the same glass, or using the same makeup. I learned all this when I used to live with my mother. We used to drink out of the same glasses, and she'd kiss me. I never caught it. I don't worry about getting it 'cause I don't have sex, not now, or use drugs."

"Not now?"

"I did it twice, but not now."

"How old were you when you had sex?"

"Last year. The same person. I was with him for a long time. But I left him, and I didn't like him anymore. He got jealous. He wouldn't let me talk to his friends or go out. I was too young for that. I decided to be by myself."

"Do you spend a lot of time alone?"

"Nah. I spend a lot of time with my friends. I have a lot of friends. I like to hang on the corner and talk to guys."

"Does your sister live with you?"

"No. I feel all right about it because I know whenever I want to see her I'm able to. I like where I live."

"If you needed to talk to someone, who would you go to?"

"It depends what happens. I would go to the right person who could help me. Either I would go to my best friend, Angela, or I'd go to my guardian. Someone would help me. I don't think they'd turn me away."

Suddenly, Raquel seemed anxious, a state of eager, nervous imbalance, holding my attention by bowing her head, and I anticipated that she would test my sense of disbelief about a crisis, then throw it back in my face.

She said, "I met the Martinez family a year ago. They didn't have much, but I like them. I began to have sex with Ricardo, who was eighteen. I guess I fell in love with him. I'm not sure. He never hurt me or nothin'. So I thought he was great. Well . . . I'm pregnant. I don't know what to do. I feel pressure and stuff. I don't know whether to kill the baby. I guess it's not killing. His mother is Pentecostal, and says it's a sin. Ricardo's got two other children by two other girls. He says that virgins are best, and he's always lookin' for kids. I have an appointment to go to an abortion clinic next week, but I don't know whether I'll go through with it." She ended the meeting abruptly saying, "I don't feel good. I gotta go."

Raquel didn't appear at the center for months, and my attempts to reach her were completely frustrated. There is nothing poetic in her loss: running across the bedraggled backdrop of El Barrio, as if being a child was a criminal activity in a country stupefied by poverty, as if she were an outsider who cannot find any point of entry into human society. She reappeared at the center with great intensity and enthusiasm, pushing a stroller with her two-month-old baby. But the counselor told me that her voice soon reflected an emptiness and her face showed the despair of her present life. The counselor held her breath in fear that she would not be able to sustain a hopeful ideal of innocence when faced with the reality of an externalized version of Raquel's inner life; she only hoped for inspiration to be able to transmute life from crisis.

Chapter 5

Angel

The fact that illness is associated with the poor—who are, from the perspective of the privileged, aliens in one's midst—reinforces the association of illness with the foreign: with an exotic, often primitive place.

Susan Sontag, *AIDS and Its Metaphors*

It was autumn and a breeze created a convolution of motion with a whirlpool of leaves whisking through the trees—the circularity of motion distracted us as we walked through Fort Tryon Park located in the north end of Manhattan's Washington Heights community. We found a haven high above the park in The Cloisters, the Metropolitan Museum of Art's medieval branch, a monastery housing the famous Unicorn Tapestries. We sat in a small room in a building enclosing a large courtyard, a sheltered arcade, overlooking the skyline. The room was darkened to protect centuries-old tapestries from the ultraviolet sun glare. On one wall was a panel of the Virgin and Child, surviving from the fourteenth century, the child on her lap, blessing with his right hand. Seated on a lion-head throne, she wears the Byzantine crown. Another wall featured a fragment of a fresco depicting the heads of angels. Most prominent was the famous Unicorn Tapestry from a series of fifteenth-century Franco-Flemish tapestries, woven of silk and wool with silver threads, remarkable for the profusion of realistic detail.

Angel would only agree to meet me in a public place, somewhere neutral, which would not have been my preference, but I accepted the terms even though it seemed controlling, frustrating, and somewhat puzzling. Angel was a six-foot-four-inch, 18-year-old Latino, with a self-confident demeanor, somewhat an impersonation of an adult. He projected an exaggerated assuredness that made me suspect that there was in fact no certainty; instead, he was managing a variety of impersonations—not a self, but a troupe of internalized players, a permanent company of characters to be called on when a self was required. He spoke from the back of his throat, creating a baritone-like impression of a television anchorman, presenting his nightmarish life with detachment, appearing to be solid, imperturbable, and maddeningly sane. He seemed almost robotic, but the most expressive of robots as he recalled memories of his mother, Angelina, whom he described as having a face so tired and leathery, she was like an old shoe.

His mother died when he was 15 years old, so he had clear memories of her. He described her as thin, nervous, and high-strung. They fought continuously; he had become a surrogate partner and their confrontations were desperate and ludicrously uncivilized. She was an active intravenous substance user from puberty until her death at 32. For fear of insanity, he presented himself as spirited, confident, and overly intense. The picture of their life was a revved-up picture of convoluted double crosses.

Their life was also about bureaucratic dehumanization, at times funny and a little eerie. He remembered the modern corridors of the offices of Human Resources, where the flickering lights suggested something almost supernaturally impersonal. The case manager was a worrying and hand-wringing type. There was always something bubbling inside Angelina—heroin or booze or pills, a cocktail of substances that added to her natural hissing. Angel's soul-sickness made him practically stiff from repressed annoyance, then alternately he became infantile, then flirtatious, with his perfectly groomed, mustachioed upper lip turned up in a lecherous sneer, his dark eyes shining with the skittish naughtiness of a teenage voluptuary. His oblique account was punctuated with moralistic conventions, making his dialogue painstakingly tedious and misleading because he was masking suffering with sanctimonious speech-making.

To help him relax, I started with some general questions. Angel was seventeen years old and was born in The Bronx. He is in the eleventh grade. "I'm going to go to college to become a doctor because I want to be in a helping profession. I want to help people.

I think that's the one area where I can be most beneficial. I like to deal with people, I don't like computers. I will be the first of my family of many generations to receive a college education: my mother never finished high school and my father only made it through the eighth grade."

I asked, "Is there anything in your life that influenced your wanting to be a doctor?"

"I would have to say it was a number of things. One being my family: my grandmother being ill, my mother and aunt dying. I always felt incapable, out-of-control; in helping them I would always see people suffering around me at a very early age. I felt it would be best for me to help people to try to have a better life. This is what brought me to the medical profession." After a few pensive moments, he added: "I describe myself as hopeful. It really depends, because some people lean toward optimism and some toward pessimism. I'm realistic. When someone says they can do this, I look at it with problems and with no problems. I try to look at things whole and balanced. It's important to me because people say, 'Oh, you can do this,' but they never mention the things that might get in the way of your doing it. So I try to see it not just the good and the bad.

"Sometimes in school with my grades, I'm really curious to see what I've gotten. With my writing, I'm curious to see what's resulting from it. My basic attitudes at school or work that I deal with . . . I'm just curious about a lot of things so I can make a wise judgment. It depends on the situation. I'm not always anxious. It doesn't overpower me or get out of hand.

"Even though I'm in a new environment now, a foster home, it's not a family setting. It's not there. It's not a realistic thing to want. You have to make do with what you have. Actually, I'm very content there."

"Can you tell me about your parents?"

"When I was born, she didn't want a baby boy, she wanted a baby girl. That whole situation evolved to her leaving me with people in the street. I got some disease that I don't remember. I was going to die, but my grandmother brought me to a doctor. They cleaned me up and gave me medicine. I was on the streets for eight or nine months. The first eight or nine months of my life, I was out on the streets. As an infant. I was told later that I would sit in my own excrement for days. At that stage of life an infant is very fragile. It must have been a gift from God. I believed I survived because of the part I was to play with my family as I got older. I took on so much responsibility because I was the only male with six women. I starting taking care of them at age six or seven. I know people say, 'What could you have done at age six or seven?' Well, in a family such as mine with many things happening . . . When I was two or three, when my cousin was born, I changed her diapers and cleaned up in the house. At five or six, I would do the laundry and wash dishes, clean up the house. When I was around ten or eleven, and my grandmother was in a wheelchair at this point, I was the only one who could push her and bring her up and down stairs. I was the smallest at the time, but I was the one that did it. It was a tremendous burden. People say to me, 'I didn't have to do that.' I had a sense of debt that I owed to my grandmother. When my grandmother passed away, I took care of my cousins. I worked and did things and didn't go to school for a year. I brought in the money. When my mother passed away, I voluntarily went to a group home. I went for unique reasons because I had no living relatives. I left that situation, and I'm now living in a foster home with a single parent. It's working out well because we have good communication.

"My older cousin is going to move in with us. We spoke about it last night, and it depends on her ability to adhere to the rules. She's lived so long without a structure that it may pose difficulty for her. It was a difficult decision for me to make. For a long time I was lacking in basic necessities and needs. I'm still pondering the decision to allow her to move in. Now I've been given these things that I've been lacking and I have to give some of them up again. It's not an easy decision to make. But if she's willing to work, then I'm willing to try–it's a mutual situation."

"You mentioned that your mother died. How old were you?"

"I was fifteen."

"What helped you cope with her death?"

"I never . . . I have not dealt with my grandmother's passing. It was so traumatic that I completely blocked out the whole situation. Realistically, I know that she is gone. Idealistically, I think she's on a long, long vacation and will be coming back at any point. It's something I feel and hope will occur, but I know it's not going to happen. When I was in the group home, they didn't allow me to grieve my mother's death. They were assuming that I didn't feel. For a long time . . . I would say from 1986 through 1988, then in 1991 . . . I had put up an emotional wall. I wouldn't smile. I chose to stay distant, but then over time, I began opening up. Now, I enjoy myself more and enjoy life. I'm not sitting in the grief that surrounded me. For about fifteen years someone around me had died consecutively with the exception of 1990. I had actually told my mother when my aunt passed away in 1989 that someone died year after year. She said, 'I won't do that to you.' She didn't have the power to hold off her death, but it helped me at the time. She broke the cycle when she died in 1991. I try to accept the fact that she isn't here and isn't suffering, which has helped me the most in my grief."

"Have you ever dreamed of her?"

"Yes, I had two dreams. "Around the time my mother passed away, she passed away in May, I had a dream that I was back at the Prince George Hotel [a welfare hotel]. I was getting off the service elevator, and I found my grandmother's ID card. I picked it up and had it in my hand and walked around to our old room. The room number was 238. I was born at 2:38. To some people, it doesn't have any significance, but to me it does. That time, 2:38, was the time I was born and came into the world. The Prince George was a new stage that I had went through in my life where we were forced to live. None of us wanted to give up the pride we had in ourselves. Not to sound too cocky. You just don't want to give up the last thing that the system cannot take from you, which is your pride. Some people actually do after they've spent years in the system.

"In this dream, I knocked at the door, and my cousin answered it." She said, 'Angel, you're home! Everybody, Angel's here.' I walked in and saw my grandmother sitting on her bed, knowing she was dead. I knew this was a dream. In a way it hurt me because I was allowing myself to feel the love, at that particular moment in the dream. I came into a space where I could not see my body, but I knew. They said, Angel, Angel, don't leave us. Come with us. I felt a sensation of being pulled forward. In the dream, I said, 'This is just a dream, and I can't go.' This occurred in less than five minutes, and what was strange was when I awoke, I said if I were ever to have that dream again for the sake of curiosity and to be with them, I would go. The remarkable thing was I had my grandmother's ID card in my hand. It was placed in a box in my closet. I know I didn't get up in my sleep and go through the boxes. It was under a number of boxes, and I had no need to go get it and use it. When I woke up and had it in my hand . . . that has never happened to me before. It was a very strange feeling. But I put it out of my mind, and it was not something I dwelt on. But I do realize it did occur. So.

"And one other dream. My mother passed away on a Tuesday. That Monday night prior to her passing . . . I saw her Saturday . . . I walked into her room, and it was really cold. It almost felt like death was there. I imagine in my case having been exposed to people dying for such a long time, I have become perceptive to this. I had the feeling this thing was sitting in the room waiting. I told her goodbye. I didn't just come out and say it, but I told her I loved her. I knew that she knew she wouldn't make it past Mother's Day. She passed away on May 14. That Monday night I had a dream. I remember, I saw *Cats*, a half-year prior to this, and in the last scene where the cat was letting go of this poor tattered cat. She was going off to heaven. And that's what I saw in my dream. It was me and a women's face, but I didn't see her because she left too quickly. I didn't realize, and I put it out of my mind. When she passed away, it came back to me. I wrote a poem and consciously I didn't know what I was writing, but the following Tuesday evening I read the poem. It was about her death. It was as if I wrote about it before it happened. It gave me a strange feeling. I don't dwell on it, I think it's just something that happens.

"She suffered cardiac arrest in a hospital emergency room. She was waiting eighteen hours to be admitted. It would have been really bad if she passed away in her house because I'd go there once a week. I don't know what I may have found. I don't think it would have been very pretty. I said to her you have to go to the hospital. For once in her life she did. I used to worry where would she be . . . Would she be out on the street or in her house. It put me at somewhat of an ease to know she was at the hospital. But, sometimes it's not good to have a fear of what will happen. People say, 'You influenced her.' But, some things are beyond your influence. I know I didn't influence her to die when she did."

"Can you describe your mother to me?"

"Before she got involved in drugs, which was before I could remember, she was an eccentric person, just as her sister Paula was. Basically, she liked to do things her way, as she wanted them. She didn't conform to the standards that society places on people. She wanted to do what she thought was best for her. The main example that I can think of: her grandparents were from Germany, pure Aryans, you should only marry white people. She saw love as having no color. Many people do not like that, loving interracially was not horrible but still raised an eyebrow with people. But my mother . . . the drugs made her into a far worse person than she was, eating her from the inside out and eventually killing her. However, she did have her good moments, her brief moments of glory, but they were few and very far apart. Basically, she was a simple person. She wasn't extravagant, but she was eccentric in many things. I remember reading that you remain at the age that you start abusing heavy drugs. She started smoking marijuana at around thirteen, and I don't know when she started using heavier things. She would draw and color and sit down with a little doll and do its hair and stuff. I know that some of it was out of loneliness, but some was because she felt content with it. When I went back to her home after she passed away, I took many of her drawings. It was interesting because there was a lot of pain in them, a lot of anger, resentment— things I feel today, but I control them. Most of the drawings were abstract, not curves, but lines.

"I remember she was involved with a gang when she was in her late teens. She was a rebel without a cause. It's funny when I think about it now, each of us had different ways of verbalizing ourselves, whether they be verbal or nonverbal. I was one that would write about it. My older cousin would act about it. My mother would draw about it. My aunt would speak about it. My grandmother took everything in and didn't let it out frequently, but she let it out at times. In those brief times, she felt years of pain in that five minutes. Often, I would characterize my life as an hour of joy and a year of pain—that's more or less how my life used to be. It's changed and is not that way anymore. I have a new perception of things."

"You mentioned writing poetry, what do you write about?"

"I have a poem titled, 'Neglect Not the Children,' which expresses the cry of many children who are suffering without the acknowledgement of people. I felt someone had to write about it. It was the basis of a documentary. I wound up on the cutting room floor because the producers received funding from an agency that demanded they focus on the children they service, so only my voice is heard in the film. I was unnerved a bit, just a bit, but I don't allow things like that to get to me. As far as personal gripes go, I was told one thing in the beginning and something else occurred later. I was given credit in the beginning as the inspiration for the film; however, it would have been nice to see me on television. Every advancement I get furthers my recognition as a poet. It's not just for me—it's for the people. I believe it allows me to convey a message to the world, a message many people feel."

"Can you tell me about your mother's death?"

"She was HIV positive. She had become very thin. AIDS weakens the organ systems of the body, and as I said she had a heart attack. She had suffered a long, long time. She became weak and frail. She showed me her arm once, and it looked like some bones with skin wrapped around it—there was no muscle left. She isn't suffering now. People say that to me. It's easy to say that, but when you feel something different. . . . They're not here. It's like being allowed to feel what you feel. I choose not to euphemize any situation. I choose to be open and candid, and sober in thinking and saying how I feel. I have no problem. I've come to that now . . . Not long ago, I wouldn't say how I felt. It's all right to feel my anger, for whatever reason I have, because I have a reason to do so. It's not something I was allowed to do before. I have moved toward allowing myself to feel. I'm not hurting people by doing so: I'm not hurting myself by expressing what I have to say. I'm not so much listening to others."

"Tell me about your father."

"I don't know very much about my father. My mother and father were out of wedlock when I was born. I really couldn't tell you much because my mother didn't speak of him much. She spoke of him when I was very young, but I don't remember. I never seen him. My mother once offered to take me to an area where he used to be, but she never did. I don't know whether I was particularly anxious to do so. Sometimes, I'm curious to see him, and sometimes I've lived this long without knowing who he is, and it's not going to be something I must know like I'm going to die if I don't know. I'm content with who I am. I think it might be interesting, if he was still alive, to see what kind of person he is and get an idea of where my roots originated from. I know my mother's side but not the other half. I think it would be interesting to see him, but it's not a life or death matter. I'll survive without seeing him."

"Have you imagined anything about him?"

"I've been told, basically he came from . . . I don't know. When I speak of roots . . . I can go back to his parents and all, but it really has to do with the person that he is, how he feels about things. I did hear a saying that influenced me, 'A man is like a tree without roots. He'll . . .' How does it go? 'A man that does not know his history is a tree without roots. He'll surely die.' I think it's important because for someone to get a thorough idea of where they came from, they have to know where they originated at. Basically, I've been working on what I've been given with the family that I had. But, I'm not dwelling on the fact that he wasn't there, then I would never move on to the future. I can't allow that to happen.

"When I was nine years old I used to hang out on the stoop with my friends, watching my father and his henchman make deals, issue orders, and reap the rewards of being big fish in a small pond. I watched my father almost kill a man, but true to the code of the neighborhood, everyone told the police they saw nothing, and my father went free. So many families were destroyed by drugs, but the code was not to turn in one of your own, no matter what he did. You can't use Judeo-Christian values to understand African justice, and my people have roots there. We take care of our own and believe what goes around comes around, but not through the Anglo system of justice.

"My early relationships, role models, what have you, were to people that you'd think of as the criminal element. Everyone had been to Rikers Island prison, not many times, but in and out like a revolving door. My uncle died there under circumstances we never found out the truth. He was found hanged in his cell with his sheet: we don't know if it was other roommates or the guards, but we know it wasn't suicide. My uncle didn't believe in suicide. It may be difficult to understand, but he was a devout Catholic, despite the crime and drugs, and he would never have taken his life."

Angel hammered home the ruthlessness of prison life and the inevitable changes it produces in men who spend their lives there. There's no glamour to prison, no fetishization, and no romantic notions that penitentiaries are crucibles that fire strong men's bodies and souls. They're ugly, cruel, and brutalizing; it's clear that the men who survive inside cripple themselves to do so, even when the maiming doesn't show. Angel knows the distinctive way gang members button their shirts, the mechanics of getting tattoos or smuggling contraband within the prison—a fully realized universe, claustrophobic but complete. The outside world is hardly a factor; Angel spent precious little time there.

"These were the contradictions of my childhood, first I was mascot and errand boy to people you would have been afraid of. I would have been seduced by charm of machismo, flashy style, and the aura of wealth and authority surrounding people in my neighborhood. Even at age ten, they advised me about women, let me drive their showy cars, and entrusted me with confidences and minor jobs that hold the promise of a future full of easy money and respect. I was a punk pit bull. I changed paths when AIDS seemed to turn on everyone. I don't mean in a moralistic sense, as punishment, but everyone was getting sick and dying, and the glimpse of this shook me more than the violence that surrounded me."

"I would have found my identity in a gang, spending years together in juvenile hall and, later, in prison, completing a criminal education and hatching an ambitious plan to form a large-scale operation that will command respect both within and outside prison walls. Prison, drugs, and death. I would have become part of the gang drifting in and out of prison, dealing drugs, murdering anyone who opposes them and protecting one another from the police and other gangs. I'm certain that was my future. When my mother became too sick to even stand up, she relied on me, and I couldn't turn my back on her. I took care of her and she even verbally abused me when I cleaned her vomit. But I stood by her until she died. She never accepted me and called me a pussy boy for not deserting her. She's gone now for years, and I still hope for her acceptance of me.

I was smarter than she could have been even at ten and eleven, and she had to deal with that."

"Can you describe your current relationship to your cousins?"

"We've lived apart for a number of years now, and we've grown in different ways. It's not that I don't love them—it's that my feelings toward them have changed. I'm not around them and we're not living in such close quarters. We were exposed to various different people, and so on. And I just think . . . I get along well with them. I take Sheri out and it's well and fine when I'm there, and I think about her when I'm not there. We've changed in some ways insofar as we feel about each other. We've grown apart in some ways.

"Heidi is coming to be with me. I don't know if it will work. I'm willing to give it a shot. I love both of them very much, but when a person's not there all the time, you tend to grow and want to do different things. I'll never stop thinking about them."

"How were you disciplined by your mother?"

"Basically, my grandmother rose . . . raised me. My mother wasn't there frequently and did not know what to do. She was quite young. My grandmother raised me in a structured environment. She exposed me to the finer things in life, the arts, music, and literature. We travelled many, many places. As far as being punished, it was more . . . It would take . . . I would be punished for the slightest things. My grandmother wouldn't allow me to walk around and do as I pleased. Even at an early age, I knew what was expected of me. I didn't frequently go out of those boundaries, but I still was not a perfect child. As far as being punished, I wasn't brutally beaten or tied up or anything. You know, my grandmother might reprimand me, taking me aside and talking to me; she was more civilized in punishment. My mother, because she had so much anger at such an early age, she was physically abusive. When I was smaller than her, she was able to beat me up, but when I got older it wasn't as easy for her. When we quarrelled I wouldn't beat her, but she used to come at me with a knife or broken glass and I'd grab her, take whatever it was in her hands and let her calm down. I would have to watch her for the rest of the evening. It was early survival class. I couldn't turn my back frequently. I remember when we were living in upstate New York, and we got into an argument about her using money for alcohol instead of for food. She tried to throw a lamp at me. And then she came at me with a steak knife and stabbed me in the shoulder. She threw me out of the house, and I tried to hit through the storm door and broke it. A neighbor called a state trooper, but they're involved in their own situation and didn't want to be bothered with *simple* family problems. I'm six-foot-four-inches now; I guess I was about six feet when I was twelve years old. I was bigger than she was and broader. People immediately assumed what she was telling them was correct—that I was trying to rob the house, take money, and beat up on her. Then instead of being brought to jail, she'd then say, 'Oh, let him stay.' I'd kind of give her a look that I'd never allow her to do that again. I would never have been able to articulate my thoughts to the police at that age. But once I learned that I was able to speak, and be heard, I wasn't as easily controlled by her whenever a police officer came over. She learned, whatever it was we fought on, it wasn't just physical, it could have been verbal, because I passed her in education, my horizons were far greater than hers. . . . I'm in the eleventh grade now, but even then when I was in the fifth grade, I was exposing myself to many things. I was more capable of controlling my situation, and that was a double-edged sword. We had an interesting relationship."

"I want to ask you about your social life. Do you make friends easily?"

"I do have friends, but I'm very selective. I don't choose to be with people that . . . I don't associate myself with the wrong crowds because I don't want to be influenced. It's unnecessary because I have better things to do with my time. I'd rather deal with mature individuals rather than immature ones, and I have often gotten along better with adults than peers. But I've changed over the past two years, and I'm getting along much better with my peers than I used to because I've allowed myself to realize this pain I've had was not singularly my own—other people had went through pain. I've learned that people are there to share and give support, and I've learned to recognize that. I can make friends quickly, depending on the environment. At my new job as a peer counselor, I've made many new friends. I work on a twenty-four-hour, seven-day-a-week, telephone line for teenagers. I can give them information and referrals, but we also deal with suicidal feelings, drug abuse, and homicide. A very select group of adolescents were chosen to be counselors—out of an outrageous number of applicants. There were three thousand applicants, fifty people were in my group and it was worked down to forty people. Now my group is thirty people, which became the core group out of three thousand people. We are the founding group of this youth line. It's a fulfilling job that allows me to extend myself to my peers and offer as much help as I can. I encounter problems where I can help people who feel alone and isolated. It has helped me realize that I was not alone in my problems—now I can extend myself to people."

"Is the job ever stressful for you?"

"No."

"Never?"

"Even calls about suicide don't scare me because . . . First of all, through the training, we learned that if someone is truly thinking about suicide, you cannot stop them from doing what they want to do. If they've made up their minds, you may be able to help by giving them other options, but essentially what we learned is if someone wants to commit suicide you cannot throw them over the edge. We have done role plays over the telephone line as part of the training. We would take them as real calls, but we'd never know if they were real or not."

"Does the issue of AIDS come up on the hotline?"

"We went through AIDS training. Around the time my mother was alive, I became a local expert. I knew how the disease was contracted, transmitted, what it did to the body, how it allowed opportunistic diseases to come in, what its symptoms were, how long it took. I knew many, many things about it. I'm not as involved in it since my mother's death. I'd like to get involved in it again. It doesn't bother me; I can deal with it because it's not that I can't because it was something that affected me personally. I'm not uncomfortable with it. I have my personal feelings about how it got here. I believe it was man-made, and I feel that way for a number of reasons. I recently come to that conclusion when I took biology. Basically, a virus is a protein-capped DNA, and it can replicate itself into anything. Because it is protein it can attach itself to anything and rearrange the DNA within that cell. Not to get into chromosomes and all, but . . . Then I thought, if you think about all the disease today, man has an idea of how to deal with them; I'm not saying he has a cure. He knows what cancer is, and he knows what happens. Essentially, he has an idea of AIDS, but AIDS is too smart and knows exactly what to attack in the body. If the lungs are attacked the immune system fights back, if the brain is attacked the immune system fights back, but if the immune system is attacked, what fights for the immune system? It's too smart, I believe, to be made by nature. I don't believe it was contracted from animals. I have my own personal beliefs, but I'm not going to argue with someone about it. I believe it is killing many people needlessly, children, infants, and adults. My personal thing, now, is that I practice temperance. I think that many people should practice temperance–control over their own self. People still like to do what they want. They are their own teacher, let's put it that way. People do as they please. I think about some of my own actions when people say don't do that, and just for the sake of curiosity or wanting to know . . . Not jumping off a roof, but something within reason. You might want to see what something's like. Broaden your ideas, or whatever. That's how we learn."

"You mentioned children before, and your life experience and what you're currently doing on the hotline seems to come from your personal motivation. It's clear that children have almost virtually gone unnoticed during the epidemic. And adolescents such as yourself. The public doesn't know what the experience of losing a parent from HIV disease is like."

A week after the interview, I received a telephone call from Angel. He sounded breathless: "My godmother, Rosa, wants to meet you. Will you be willing to come to her home? She lives in The Bronx. I hope you say yes. It's important to me." Despite being puzzled by the request, I said I would go with him, and we arranged a time the following week.

The Bronx streets were teeming with swaggering hoods with their brawny preening, lustrous suits, heavy jewelry, and slicked back hair; the grumpy fruit and vegetable man; the local girls with sky-high hair, skinny heels, and tight dresses; and the cars, the social clubs, the gambling, the suave crooning from the jukeboxes, and the macho banter. It evoked my own childhood; I had grown up several blocks away. It was as if with reverent clarity and precision a window opened onto memories of the past, as it was and now as it is.

Angel greeted me at the door and took me alone into a bedroom. He began: "When I was younger, my family was basically Catholic. When I got older, I had more or less a choice of what I wanted to do. I believe in God, and I try to lead my life accordingly. I don't really care for strict religious people because they persecute others who are not of their religion. God says you're supposed to practice peace amongst yourselves. People of different religions . . . Well, when they get in the same room they say, 'You should be this. You should be that.' If it's all to the same God, you should all be practicing peace, which does not occur.

"I have a godmother, Rosa, who is a Santería priestess." He displayed a wrist bracelet of chartreuse and pale lemon-colored small beads. He continued, "This bracelet protects me from death. My godmother told me that if someone is dying in a hospital, they won't pass until the bracelet is cut from their wrist."

Santería is a religion concentrated in Cuba and other Caribbean islands, and among Hispanics in Florida and New York City. Santería (the Way of the Saints) is a syncretistic religion of Caribbean origin that combines the Gods, Goddesses, and beliefs of the Yoruba and Bantu people in Southern Nigeria, Senegal, and the Guinea Coast with the God, Saints, and beliefs of Roman Catholicism. Many of its followers are uncomfortable with the name Santería and prefer to call it *La Regla Lucumi*. Its origins date back to the slave trade when Yoruba natives were forcibly transported from Africa to the Caribbean. Upon arrival, they were typically baptized by the Roman Catholic church, and their native practices were suppressed. They developed a novel way of keeping their old beliefs alive by equating or integrating the identities of the Gods and Goddesses of their traditional religions with the Christian saints. For example, *Babalz Ayi* became St. Lazarus (patron of the sick); *Shango* became St. Barbara (controls thunder, lightning, fire); *Eleggua* or *Elegba* became St. Anthony (controls roads, gates); *Obatala* became both Our Lady of Las Mercedes and the Resurrected Christ (father of creation, source of spirituality); *Oggzn* became St. Peter (patron of war); *Oshzn* became Our Lady of Charity (controls money, sensuality).

Santería has been suppressed in Cuba since the revolution; however, it is rapidly growing elsewhere. There are believed to be 300,000 practitioners of Santería in New York alone. Many Santerían beliefs are not known outside of the faith. The deities are referred to in a similar hierarchy as other religions: for instance, God is referred to as *Olorun*, the "owner of heaven." He is the supreme deity, the creator of the universe, and of the lesser Gods called *Orisha*. Each of the latter has an associated Christian Saint, a principle, important number, color, food, dance posture, and emblem. The Orishas need food in the form of animal sacrifice and prepared dishes, as well as human praise, in order to remain effective. Santeros practice ritual sacrifice, which forms an integral part of many Santerían religious rituals. The animal's blood is collected and offered to the Orisha. Chickens are the most common animal used. Their sacrifice is believed to please the Gods, and to bring good luck, purification, and forgiveness of sins. Rhythmic sounds and feverish dancing during Santerían rituals are believed to lead to possession of the individual by the particular Orisha being invoked. The individual then speaks and acts as the Orisha.

The religion is a hierarchical system based on group-centered cooperation, using little or no proselytizing to expand the number of followers. One rises through the ranks by initiation. Age commands respect, both chronological age and time in initiatory level. For individuals undergoing an initiation process, there are major stressors because disciples spend years in preparation to enter adulthood within the religion and assume spiritual responsibility for themselves within the ocha family, and perhaps other families as well. After this initiation, the person is referred to as a priest, *yalorisha* or *babalorisha* (mother or father of the orisha in Yoruba), or santero/a in the Santería tradition.

Angel continued: "I wanted you to know that I was taking this step to become a priest because the interview wouldn't have been complete without this important side to my life. But, I don't trust many people with this information—there's a lot of prejudice and misunderstanding. I consulted with my godmother, and she wanted to meet you."

Rosa was making food in the kitchen, and when she saw Angel her face beamed with pride. She said: "I have many godchildren." She smiled at me, saying, "Maybe you will become one of them. You have trouble with your back and have been having stomach problems." I told her that it was true. She continued with her intuitive observations of me, "You have few friends. You've suffered a lot of loss. If you like I will do a reading for you." I answered in affirmation.

Angel and I shared a cab ride, and I dropped him off on a street about a mile away. I thanked him for sharing this part of his life. He admonished me to do as his godmother instructed me to do, and I clutched a paper bag filled with items given to me by Rosa, along with a list of instructions.

Chapter 6

The Uncertainty of Knowing

A millennium and a half later, their descendants, too conscientious to leave the fate of unwanted children to chance or the kindness of strangers, and too preoccupied with family ties and lineage to admire effective solutions, intervened to establish an orderly public means of handling them.

John Boswell, *The Kindness of Strangers*

I arranged to meet Julia, Jamal's biological grandmother, after several conversations with Bob and Micky, seeking their approval for such a meeting. Julia represents a two-generational family struck by HIV disease; her daughter Saudah, Jamal's mother, died from the disease during the first months of his infancy. This part of The Bronx, called Morrisania, is on very high ground. Off 165th Street, around the corner from The Bronx Museum of the Arts and opposite St. Simeon's Episcopal Church built in the beginning of this century, a staircase rises to a street two stories up, like something you'd climb in Montmartre. From there you can see the new mall, a few blocks east of the stadium, on 161st Street: it has a Waldbaum's supermarket, a multiplex cinema, and a food court— just like the suburbs. Rich people lived here in the early 1900s, in fancy apartment buildings with gracious courtyards, across from a park where a fountain dedicated to Heinrich Heine teems with sea imagery; though the fountain is dry, and the mermaids have lost their heads.

Nearby on Morris Avenue is a throwback to pre-Frigidaire America: an icehouse where you can buy ice in 300-pound blocks. The most historic building near the stadium is not The Bronx County

Courthouse, with its friezes of working people, but the Concourse
Plaza Hotel, where every Democratic Presidential candidate
through Kennedy attended the Ladies' Democratic Club Lunch,
now a residence for senior citizens and the disabled. It's all still
here, under the litter and graffiti, except the rich people, of course.

Jamal's was an open adoption so that he knows his biological
mother and family of origin, and he and his adoptive father maintain
contact. Julia is Jamal's grandmother–he's named after her. She
raised Jamal from infancy for two years, becoming the court-
appointed guardian when her daughter, Saudah, was mandated to a
drug rehabilitation facility in upstate New York. She didn't complete
the treatment program, leaving after three weeks to return to sex
work to support her addiction to speedballing, the injection use of a
combination of heroin and cocaine. Saudah never revealed the identity of Jamal's biological father and may not actually know who the
father is. Her contact during Jamal's infancy was intermittent and
unpredictable, although Julia acknowledges that a mother-infant
bond between them was apparent. Eventually, Julia sought legal
guardianship to protect Jamal from Saudah, whose visits became
increasingly disturbing and out of control. She was banned from
Julia's home through a painful act of "tough love" after one Christmas when most of the painstakingly wrapped presents disappeared
from beneath the tree. Jamal's presents of toys and clothing were
gone. A gold cross with a diamond in the center–which Julia was
going to send to Clifton, her former husband, who was imprisoned–
was also taken.

The three-room apartment occupied by Julia and her sister Yvette
was painted a tenement green throughout, several shades too dark
given the lack of light. The living room windows revealed the
skeletal facade of a burned-out building, conveying the image of a
war zone. In this section of The Bronx, guns discharge throughout
the day and residents get caught in the cross fire within their apart-
ments. I heard a popping sound that either could have been a car
backfiring or gunshot, and I remembered a mother on a 6:00 p.m.
television newscast saying that, at times, her family crawled along
the floor in their home. The apartment was furnished with hand-me-
downs from her grandmother, and each room had an item from a
1930's post-deco, maple bedroom set too large to be grouped to-

gether. We sat at a chrome and formica kitchen table, the chairs covered in coral vinyl. Julia served a cup of Bustelo coffee, a dense, bitter-tasting brand popular with Latinos.

Julia raised her hands to cover her face, revealing a small, faded, and primitively drawn tattoo of a cross on her palm between her thumb and first finger. The tattoo was incongruous with her general appearance, which was unremarkably conventional; the tattoo insinuated the former life of destruction and chaos. Julia was incarcerated for two years for drug possession and for being an accessory to armed robbery. She was introduced to both intravenous heroin use and criminality by her former husband, Clifton, who is currently imprisoned, doing time for gun possession and armed robbery.

"If it wasn't Cliff, it would've been someone else. It was a matter of time. But, it was him, so he bears the brunt of my anger about the progression of my addiction. He's a veteran addict, someone who shot up, survived, and remained HIV negative. Younger addicts turned to crack and snorting heroin during the 1980s when gossip circulated about friends. It would've been difficult to dismiss when you witnessed people deteriorate and drop dead before your eyes. So that rumor of the epidemic spreading in the injection-using community was widespread. We tried to fool ourselves, believing that the multiple deaths were from bad dope and overdoses. In our hearts we knew."

After serving her sentence, Julia was resolute about not returning to a life of criminality and substance use. She attended Narcotics Anonymous (NA) meetings in the penitentiary and remained clean and sober after release. She found out she was HIV seropositive after being diagnosed with pneumocystis cariini pneumonia (PCP), the most common opportunistic infection associated with HIV disease.

"Cliff will probably never make it. He's completely caught in addiction. While I'm alive there are desires that drugs can't give me, but Cliff doesn't know he's suffering. He grits his teeth, but there's fear, lies, and more lies, to himself most importantly. He'll be out on parole in six months. I'm oppressed by a certain memory of long ago; I have hundreds of such memories—the demons—hundreds of memories. He's part of the past. I can't blame him for getting me into IV drugs. If it wasn't him it would have been someone else, or me.

"I was on the brink for years, so it wouldn't have taken much persuasion, but it did represent crossing the line. It titillated Cliff, like I was an innocent, a virgin, or something. You know what I mean. It was sexual and it changed our sex together: I think fucking became about life and death, and we devoured each other. I remember feeling differently about him, too. I felt rescued in a peculiar way: copping dope, sharing it, exchanging needles, is like a breast-feeding baby, that's how intimate it becomes. But, don't get me wrong, getting drugs and getting high is not unconditional love. It's a distortion of life-giving, the other side of the coin.

"I went upstate once to see him. The bus ride was seven hours; the prison was on the Canadian border, far from the streets of Brooklyn, away from anyone who knows him. When I saw the complex of buildings, they loomed as a threat to humanity. I broke into a cold sweat and thought I was going to pass out.

"Cliff seemed unrecognizable, a stranger, to me on the visit. I was sober in NA only six months at the time, and my program friends advised against my seeing him. They thought I'd be too vulnerable, that he'd influence me. I didn't want anyone's permission. It tormented me to think of him alone in prison. I thought no one else was like me, and I was like no one else. I felt alone. I had to go. I was no longer the same person, six months into sobriety, and the top of my head was blown away.

"Cliff was high. If you want drugs, there's always a way. I remember feeling squeamish, seeing him stoned. My God! We used together for years–we didn't never use. During sex, during dinner, always. He'd cop dope for me. I'd give him the money after a long day's waitressing. I worked, I was able to work, even though there were incidents in the diner. Some asshole, a mongrel hanger-on came on to me once, and I purposely spilled a hot cup of coffee in his lap. I never flaunted myself, although there were times I got paid for sex; sometimes they were customers in the diner. But I never remembered them: I put it out of my mind. He could've been a trick. So what, I remember thinking, 'Get lost. Who gives you the right.' My attitudes were so distorted, even though most of the men I had sex with were pigs, but I hold myself accountable for my behavior, that's what I've learned in NA."

Clifton is Malcolm's biological father, but Julia's other child, Saudah, was conceived during a one-night stand. "I don't remember much about Saudah's father. I think she was the result of sex during a blackout, so I can't be sure of the father, though I remember someone vaguely, but it could've been someone else. Cliff was in the tombs for several days, and we were trying to get him a lawyer or bail or just out. He was caught grabbing some woman's purse . . . an old woman. God, she probably had a walker, nothing could deter Cliff, especially some pushover. And, well, he had a gun. I was going through bad withdrawal and needed a fix really bad. I was on a run. I never copped for myself; I always depended on Cliff. I met this dope fiend in a bar. I never considered myself a dope fiend, even though I was, because there were things I wouldn't do—not many, but enough to keep some sense of self-respect. I suppose that's the dictionary definition of denial. I spotted this guy and knew he'd be able to get me a bag. I was shaking and feared that I'd go into a seizure. He seemed a sure bet. I remember leaving the bar with him, going back to his room at the Corinthian—this fleabag hotel where junkies, former junkies, and methadone maintenance types lived. The last thing I remember was a couple of his friends in the room and all of us shooting up. So he could have been the father, or it could've been someone else. Maybe her father was the dealer. I don't even remember having sex. It may not have been sex, but rape. I bled the next day and could barely walk. It's no wonder that Saudah was an addict—it's in her genetic code."

There are times when Julia believes that we're all prisoners, some behind the iron bars, others facing the barriers of social circumstance. She took a trip to prison before making the adoption decision, but she acknowledges, "There was still an uncertainty to me knowing. I didn't want to put aside what I knew. I had done that all my life. I needed to see Cliff." The visit with Clifton was a spiritual awakening. Julia recognizes that if you can't endure looking at yourself, someone else can serve as a mirror reflection. She understood a particular irrationality circumscribed her love for Cliff. At times, she explored her consciousness, remembering a few tender or nurturing moments and memorizing those easily accessible occasions to cherish when despairing of her life. Her subconscious dreamscape annihilated those memories with images of male familial sexual abuse and incest, and intimacy with Cliff became transformed by symbols of drug use, as needle-sharing substituted for intercourse. Julia appreciates the bizarre irony of HIV infection. "It wasn't until I discovered my HIV status that I got clean by joining NA and going into therapy. I guess I would have died on the streets or in prison. I got my life back and confronted my mortality at the same time. I took unimaginable risks with my life and didn't give a shit: I felt like a piece of shit."

Julia, her eyes reddened with tears, reached for another tissue, adding it to the ball of others that she fingered anxiously. She continued by describing with halting speech, interrupting herself when the pain was insufferable, how she arrived at the decision to place Jamal up for adoption. "I believed taking care of Jamal kept me alive. We love each other. When we were away in the country this weekend we lay on the grass together, and I felt the grandeur of the universe. It's just that simple. He's my purpose: It's my unfinished work on this planet. There's no one who can take care of him like me. No one. Sure, Cliff says not to worry, he'll be fine, but he's not going to be the one responsible for him."

Julia acknowledges the strong bond between Jamal and her sister Yvette. "Yvette was angry with me for not considering her as Jamal's guardian before I placed him up for adoption. I had convincing doubts about her ability to provide for him, and I couldn't discuss them without both of us getting crazy. I thought I'd lose her and be all alone–the threat from her was a powerful wedge. But I had to consider Jamal first."

Julia speaks of the "slow" disease process of HIV. There are times when she wishes it were over, feeling that "giving up" would be preferable. Then she witnesses herself struggling to hold on to life, to be present in Jamal's life. "I feel guilt and shame since I wasn't there for my children–all the years of drugs and running the streets. There are times when I can't stand it anymore, and it's too much for me."

It took Julia a year, until Jamal was two years old, to decide to give him up for adoption, and it became the focus of her psychotherapy, which she was receiving without fee from an AIDS community agency. "I felt such tension, and I did since he was born. But it became more painful when Jamal turned two. I had 100

T cells then, 27 T cells now. That's it, 27. I guess it's a miracle that I'm still alive. Shit. My platelet count is down and I lost fifteen pounds over the last two months. The weight loss is the most difficult part because I think that people can tell I have AIDS. I think that people are staring at me—that I have the 'look.' I have nosebleeds that won't stop because my platelet count is low. At least I don't have my periods since the hysterectomy, which was HIV related. I developed cervical cancer, and that's common for HIV-positive women."

Julia didn't know that Jamal was going to be placed with gay parents, although it was an open adoption. She was able to meet the prospective adoptive parents, but the agency retained all rights of approval. At first, she was fiercely opposed to Jamal being placed with gay male parents. She has Pentecostal roots, although her family, when they migrated to New York City from South Carolina, wandered from the fundamentalism of their church background. But the aversion toward lesbians and gay men prevailed, despite a lesbian relationship she experienced during incarceration. She recollected favorably the woman who befriended her in prison: "I was terrified in prison, feeling abandoned and depressed. Lucy held me and I needed desperately to be held. At first, there was nothing sexual. She didn't hit on me—we became friends. Even when it was sexual, I never thought of it as a lesbian relationship because we were friends, and I knew it was temporary. I rarely think of her. I guess I put it away and out of my mind."

Julia met Bob the first time in the offices of the adoption agency. She admitted being prepared for battle after formulating a list of objections, foremost that Jamal required an unmistakably powerful male role model. There were cognizant objections, but the unconscious antipathy was insidious. She liked Bob because he presented himself confidently, comfortable in his racial and sexual identity and determined to be a father regardless of the scrutiny of his character. She couldn't avoid conceding that he impressed her on every count. There were more unanswerable questions after Julia left the meeting. She returned home with a fierce headache, and the following day she was spent from a restless night without sleep. There was no one who could counsel her, there were no books to read; instead, she wrestled with her conscience and the best interests of her child. She knew there were incalculable risks and that Bob was the most suitable choice. "I wanted to protect Jamal in the ways that I couldn't for my children, in ways that I wasn't protected. I believed having a gay father would be an additional burden, and imagining not being alive and part of his life was intolerable. There would be an uncertainty with any adoption, but I knew that I had to choose Bob. It was a gut decision."

Julia described grappling with a moral dilemma and the pragmatism of materialistic considerations–Bob would be the most suitable provider of a comfortable environment. He was educated and had lucrative employment. He was African American, so Jamal would not suffer a cultural diaspora. It wasn't until she resolved the moral question that she was comfortable with her decision to place Jamal. She had already disposed of often contradictory etiologic and psychological theories of same-sex relatedness. "I finally accepted that no one knew whether people were born that way or choose. It was my religious beliefs that affected me the most, and I couldn't seek counsel from a Pentecostal clergyman because the answer was clear. It was more open between myself and God. The answer came quite simply, and I was at peace."

During our interview I observed Julia wane, and she appeared to age when the interview was about to conclude. She wore the countenance of AIDS. She reached for my hand, her eyes on the verge of a question, longing for assurance that she had made the correct decision. She retracted her hand and question in a distinct stroke, excusing herself to rest by thanking me for visiting her.

Chapter 7

Voices from the Past

You said, "They're harmless dreamers and they're loved by the people."–"What," I asked you, "is harmless about a dreamer, and what," I asked you, "is harmless about the love of the people?–Revolution only needs good dreamers who remember their dreams."

Tennessee Williams, *Camino Real*

Since the 1960s, several variations on the family unit have emerged. More unmarried couples are living together, before or instead of marrying. Some elderly couples, most often widowed, are finding it more economically practical to cohabit without marrying. Homosexual couples also live together as a family more openly today, sometimes sharing their households with the children of one partner or with adopted or foster children. Communal families, made up of groups of related or unrelated people, have long existed in isolated instances. Such units began to occur in the United States during the 1960s and 1970s as an alternative lifestyle, but by the 1980s the number of communal families was diminishing.

All industrial nations are experiencing family trends similar to those found in the United States. The problem of unwed mothers–especially very young ones and those who are unable to support themselves–and their children is an international one, although improved methods of birth control and legalized abortion have slowed the trend. Divorce is increasing even where religious and legal impediments to it are strongest.

Unchecked population growth in developing nations threatens the family system. The number of surviving children in a family has rapidly increased as infectious diseases, famine, and other causes of child mortality have been reduced. Because families often cannot support so many children, the reduction in infant mortality has posed a challenge to the nuclear family and to the resources of developing nations. Increasing proportions of never-married mothers were being found in all regions and most socioeconomic groups across the country in 1992. About 24 percent of single women age 18 to 44 had borne a child (as of June 1992), compared with 15 percent a decade earlier. The proportion of single mothers more than doubled among women with one or more years of college (4.4 percent in 1982; 11.3 percent in 1992) and nearly doubled among women with a high school diploma (17.2 percent in 1982; 32.5 percent in 1992). The proportion of single mothers among women who did not complete high school was also higher in 1992 (48.4 percent) than in 1982 (35.2 percent). Out-of-wedlock childbearing increased among all racial and ethnic groups between 1982 and 1992. About two-thirds (67 percent) of births to black women in 1992 were out of wedlock, compared with 27 percent for Hispanic women and 17 percent for white women. Comparable figures in 1982 were 49 percent, 16 percent, and 10 percent, respectively. In 1992, about 65 percent of teenage (15 to 19 years old) births were out of wedlock. Ninety-four percent of black American teenage births were out of wedlock, compared with 60 percent of Hispanic and 56 percent of white teenage births.

According to the Bureau of the Census, United States Department of Commerce, less than half the nation's 68.1 million families had children present in the home in 1993. The most recent year in which most families included children was 1982. Two-parent families accounted for 36 percent of family households in 1993, down from 50 percent in 1970. There were about 28.2 million nonfamily households in 1993, most of which were one-person households. People living alone made up 84 percent of the nonfamily households in the nation. The number of unmarried-couple households was 3.5 million in 1993, seven times larger than the number of such households in 1970 (523,000). Single parents in 1993 headed nearly 30 percent of all family groups with children, a significant increase from 12 percent in 1970. A child in a one-parent situation was just somewhat more likely to be living with a divorced parent (37 percent) in 1993 than with a never-married parent (35 percent). A decade earlier, a child was twice as likely to be living with a divorced parent as with a never-married parent.

Single mothers raising children outnumbered single fathers raising children by six to one. Although two-thirds of all single parents were white, one-parent situations were much more common among black Americans than whites. About 63 percent of all black family groups with children were maintained by single parents, versus 25 percent of comparable white family groups. Among Hispanics, single parents represented 35 percent of family groups with children.

The nuclear family was the most common preindustrial unit of social organization: both urbanization and industrialization changed family structure. The modern family contrasts with earlier forms in function, composition, life cycle, and, significantly, in the roles of husbands and wives. The only function that endures is the provision of affection and emotional support, particularly to infants and young children. Institutions perform functions the agrarian family once did, such as economic production, education, religion, and recreation. Jobs are usually separate from the family group; family members often work in different occupations and in locations away from the home. Education is provided by the state or by private groups. Religious training and recreational activities are available outside the home, although both still have a place in family life. The family is still responsible for the socialization of children. Even in this capacity, however, the influence of peers and of the mass media has assumed a larger role.

Family composition in industrial societies has changed dramatically. The average number of children born to a woman in the United States, for example, fell from 7.0 in 1800 to 2.0 by the early 1990s. Consequently, the number of years separating the births of the youngest and oldest children has declined. This has occurred with increased longevity. In earlier times, marriage normally dissolved through the death of a spouse before the youngest child left home. Today husbands and wives potentially have about as many years together after the children leave home as before.

Some of these developments relate to ongoing changes in women's roles. Women in all stages of family life have joined the labor force. Rising expectations of personal gratification through marriage and family, combined with relaxed legal grounds for divorce and increasing employment opportunities for women, have contributed to a rise in the divorce rate in the United States and elsewhere. In 1986, for instance, there was approximately one divorce for every two marriages in the United States.

During the twentieth century, extended family households have declined in prevalence. This change is associated particularly with increased residential mobility and with diminished financial responsibility of children for aging parents, as pensions from jobs and government-sponsored benefits for retired people became more common. By the 1970s, the prototypical nuclear family yielded to modified family units including the one-parent family, the stepfamily, and the childless family. One-parent families in the past were usually the result of the death of a spouse. Now, however, most one-parent families are the result of divorce, although some are created when unmarried women bear children. In 1991, more than one out of four children lived with only one parent, usually the mother.

Typical America is composed of many racial and ethnic groups. In 1994, almost 26 million Americans (9.9 percent) were of Hispanic origin, and more than 9 million Americans (3.5 percent) identified themselves as Asian-Pacific Islanders. Blacks numbered 32.5 million, or 12.5 percent of the population, and the American Indian/ Eskimo/Aleut populations made up about 2.2 million (0.8 percent). An estimated 192.5 million people (74.1 percent) considered themselves white non-Hispanic.

There has been a steep rise in out-of-wedlock births, changing the definition of family. According to the 1992 census, 70 percent of African-American women and 22 percent of white women ages 15 to 34 have a first child before their first marriage. In 1960, the figures were 42 percent of African-American women and 9 percent of white women.

The U.S. Census Bureau counts 1.6 million same-sex couples living together. Of 1,200 randomly selected adults in a research study, only 22 percent chose the legal definition of family in favor of a broader and more emotional definition. In another survey of 877 fathers in Los Angeles, Washington, Denver, Louisville, and Omaha, about one in forty considered themselves either gay or bisexual. In 1985, New Jersey found that homelessness of families was the primary or secondary factor for placement of 40 percent of youths in foster care.

In July 1989, the New York State Court of Appeals ruled that a gay man whose long-term partner had died qualified as a family. The survivor was therefore entitled to assume the lease of his partner's rent-controlled Manhattan apartment. Similar state legislation and municipal ordinances are under consideration nationwide. Legislators, judges, and elected officials are forging efforts to reach an all-inclusive understanding of the family.

The debate on lesbian and gay families successfully deflected attention from other components of multiculturalism—it was the red herring that defeated the entire curriculum.

The dispute on multiculturalism in New York City along with the growing number of judicial custody decisions throughout the country propelled lesbian and gay families into the national print and electronic media spotlight. During one week in September 1993 alone, *Time*, *The New York Times*, and several television talk shows reported on lesbian and gay parents. In Henrico County, Virginia, Circuit Court Judge Bulford Parsons Jr. ruled that Sharon Bottoms, a lesbian, was an unfit parent, and awarded custody of her two-year-old son, Tyler, to Bottoms' mother. Parsons accompanied his judgment with personal disapprobation. To support his ruling, the judge cited a case concerning a woman who had granted her husband custody of their daughter but then sued to reclaim her when she found out her husband was gay. Siding with the woman, the court had declared that "the conditions under which this child must live daily are not only unlawful but they also impose an intolerable burden on her." Judge Parsons' one reason for his ruling was Sharon's lesbianism. Virginia is just one of four states where legal precedent deems lesbian and gay parents unfit (Arkansas, Missouri, and North Dakota are the others). Only New Hampshire and Florida categorically bar gays as adoptive parents. By contrast, in Washington, DC, local officials held a seminar in 1993 to instruct lesbians and gay men on how to adopt.

The Vermont Supreme Court and the Commonwealth of Massachusetts Appeals Court each heard cases in which a lesbian asked to become the adoptive parent of her partner's children. The decisions will be the nation's first appellate-level decisions on the issue. For years, lesbians and gay men sought court sanction for their right to parent. In 1989, in Newark, Ohio, an Appeals Court overruled the adoption of a seven-year-old boy placed into the home of two gay male partners. In 1988, in Boulder, Colorado, the Department of Social Services approved an application filed by a lesbian to adopt a child.

For the twenty-fifth anniversary of the first Gay Liberation organization, founded after the Stonewall Rebellion in 1969, I was invited to speak at New York University and delivered a speech titled, "The Ethics of Caregiving: On the Occasion of the 25th Anniversary Reunion of Gay Liberation Front (GLF)."[1] It seems fitting to include this speech in this book because it highlights the longing of lesbians and gay men to be parents. During the HIV disease epidemic, lesbians and gay men have been thrust into a primary caregiving role, and a number of them have transmuted the experience of painful loss into giving life-sustenance to orphans left behind by deceased parents. The following is the text of that speech.

*   *   *

Sisters and Brothers, I am deeply moved to be sitting here on the occasion of the twenty-fifth anniversary reunion of Gay Liberation Front (GLF). I must thank Jim Clifford, a brother in the authentic meaning of the term, for having the tenacity and energy to organize this event.

I have always been gay; my earliest memories are filled with homoerotic images: Flash Gordon, James Dean, Robert Reggio (a grammar school mate). My fantasies were about rescue, most often Hollywood romantic. My yearnings were lyrical, often in the music of liberation, Aretha Franklin and Nina Simone. I wasn't openly gay as a child–I knew about shame. Out, no; identifiable, yes. In other words, they called me names; [I was] beaten, humiliated, gossiped about, shunned as contagio[us], and treated with hormone therapy.

Still an adolescent, I was first in Students for a Democratic Society (SDS). Then, in my early twenties, the antiwar movement. I was a community organizer during the late 1960s on New York's Lower East Side and was the editor of a bilingual newsletter, *Basta!*, printed on a hand-operated mimeograph machine, which my life partner, Michael, and I handed out on street corners. I was on the staff of

I-Kon, a magazine that owned a bookstore on East 4th Street. It was a politic I believed in, but it was not about my core identity.

In 1969, I was a drug addiction counselor at Odyssey House on East 6th Street. Dr. Judith Densen-Gerber confronted me along with other staff, including a gay psychologist, for being gay. Point blank, they told me to begin psychotherapeutic treatment—the sole reason: I was a gay man. If I declined, they would terminate my employment. I refused and they fired me.

Within a month, the Stonewall Rebellion occurred. I joined Gay Liberation Front that summer. I was on the editorial collective of the first new-wave gay liberation newspaper, *Come Out!* I was photographed for the *Come Out!* poster, photographed by Peter Hujar, running down a Lower West Side street with other GLFers, which was to become emblematic of the new gay movement for twenty-five years. I would like to reclaim my nameless representation: I am Steven Dansky, in the striped shirt, second from right, genetically gay at conception, antisexist by choice, unconditionally "Out of the Closet."

When, in 1970, I wrote the controversial article, "Hey Man," it became one of the earliest theoretical articles from the contemporary gay liberation movement. The essay, published widely in the United States and worldwide, formulated the primacy of gay men raising children. "Hey Man" proposed that gay male collectives assume "the responsibility of adopting and raising male homeless children."[2]

The idea of gay men raising children was unique for several reasons. It confronted head on the profound segregation of gay men from children based on societal and internalized homophobic notions that sexual identity is synonymous with the propensity toward pedophilia. I believed nurturing through childraising essential to any integrated, life-affirming gay identity. "Hey Man" also attempted to align with the principles of feminism and promote a shift from total to shared responsibility for childraising. The essay was visionary, aspiring beyond civil libertarian goals: before the publication of "Hey Man," gay male collectives didn't exist, and within a year, they appeared in every major U.S. city as an alternative to the traditional biological family unit.

By 1972, Kenneth Pitchford, John Knoebel, and myself wrote "The Effeminist Manifesto" stating the following principle:

Our first and most important step, however, must be to take upon ourselves at least our own share of the day-to-day, life-sustaining drudgery that is usually consigned to women alone. To be useful in this way can release women to do other work of their own choosing and can also begin to redefine gender for the next generation. Of paramount concern here, we ask to be included in the time-consuming work of raising and caring for children, as a duty, a right, and a privilege.[3]

Effeminism was a movement by men who were committed to anti-sexism. Men who were profeminists no matter their sexual identity, gay, heterosexual, bisexual, or asexual, were invited to join this new effort that departed from other male-dominated movements, such as leftism, gay liberation, or the counterculture. Effeminists subscribed to the theory that the essence of all oppression was male supremacy—the most fundamental duality being gender used to systematize power dominance.

In the 1990s, throughout the United States, lesbian and gay families are increasingly visible not only in cities with large lesbian and gay populations, such as New York and San Francisco, as *The New York Times* reported, but also in Ypsilanti Township, Michigan; Salina, Kansas; Montclair, New Jersey; and Tacoma, Washington. There may be hundreds of thousands or even millions of lesbian and gay parents.

The changing definition of family within American culture and the stabilization of lesbian and gay partnerships, including the attempt to legally sanction same-sex domestic partnership and the incorporation of adoptive and donor-inseminated children into the household system of same-sex coparents is becoming prevalent. Figures from the annual census in 1988 indicate that fewer than 27 percent of the nation's 91 million households fit the traditional model of a family. Simultaneously, the United States Bureau of Census counted 1.6 million same-sex couples living together, up from 1.3 million in 1970.

There are nearly half a million foster children in the United States. The emotional consequences of foster care—of being moved from one home to another, from foster family to institution and back—on any child are unpredictable. The damage that has been inflicted on generations of families and the legacy of institutional abuse and neglect presents a haunting portrait of children growing up without childhood.

Also, social definitions of family have evolved, along with several landmark legal developments that expanded the meaning of what constitutes a family. In May 1989, San Francisco's Board of Supervisors passed domestic partnership legislation recognizing lesbian and gay male couples as families. The ordinance, which was put on the ballot for a referendum, defines domestic partnership as "two people who have chosen to share one another's lives in an intimate and committed relationship of mutual caring." The American family is changing, with fewer than 27 percent of the nation's 91 million households in 1988 fitting the traditional models of a family.

Race coalesced with lesbian and gay politics when the New York City Board of Education proposed a rainbow curriculum of multicultural education. The reaction from certain communities brought fierce opposition, eventually resulted in the dismissal of the Board's Chancellor, Joseph Fernandez. Opposition centered on that section of the curriculum that addressed lesbian and gay families and included a reading list for teachers on the subject.

An astronomical $500 million has been paid by the American Roman Catholic church in settlements for claims of child sexual abuse at the hands of the male clergy. Information about each case, as reported in *Time*, has been restricted to a small circle of church officials at the Vatican. The church even disputes whether or not sexual abuse is a moral question. Rome prefers to view it only as a moral violation of the celibacy commitment. They don't talk about pedophilia. They talk about celibacy.

My life work is to pro-create, beyond biological constraints, to refuse to be segregated from the lives of children. Thank you, Blake, Erica, Sheri, Amy, Justin, and Zachary. I believe the next decade of lesbian and gay political struggle will focus on children—the raising and care of children by lesbian and gay men. We have a special responsibility to participate in this struggle, in demonstrations, in courts, and at the bassinet. We must also continue to persevere to have the history/herstory of out people included in the educational curricula from grammar to graduate school—not only two mommies/daddies, but how we make art through Michelangelo/Bonheur, music through Tchaikovsky/Smith, poetry though Whitman/Rich, and literature through Baldwin/Stein. This is the story of our life.

Now to Glennon, Steven, Aris, Sandy, JoAnne, Kenny, José, Brian, and Darren.

In a speech given by Larry Kramer, he said, as I quoted in my book, *Now Dare Everything: Tales of HIV-Related Psychotherapy*, "There's got to be a higher vision for your reason for being. You've got to want to end this!" My roots are in longtime activism, political writing, and poetry. To be quite up front, my higher vision proceeds from an enduring, lifelong commitment to struggle against all manifestations of oppression, and this is what brought me to work in the fight against the HIV/AIDS epidemic.

A couple of years into the epidemic, after serving at Gay Men's Health Crisis (GMHC) (where I served continuously as a volunteer for eight years from 1983 to 1991), I returned to school in a graduate social work program, driven by grievous necessity. In my book *Now Dare Everything: Tales of HIV-Related Psychotherapy*, I recounted the stark transition of my life during the beginning of the pandemic by saying, "It is almost inconceivable to remember life before the epidemic . . . The epidemic transformed my life, personally, politically, and professionally. Indeed, even the dominion of my subconscious tolerates dreamlike representations of suffering and losses through illness and death."[4] The other images are of caregiving. So whether it's changing an infant's diapers or an incontinent brother with end-stage AIDS, or trying to comprehend the preverbal communication of a toddler or the dysphasic language of a lover with HIV-related dementia, caregiving is all that truly matters—nothing else matters, except of course, our AIDS activism, without which many more of us would have died.

A further note on the HIV/AIDS epidemic—lesbians have been present with their total being during this holocaust. As gay men, we must support the fundamental humanity of women, including a woman's right to reproductive choice and to protection from domestic violence, the necessity for quality female health care, and the right of lesbians to parent.

To use the popular vernacular, I am a survivor. I survived the nuclear family, and William Howard Taft High School, the patriarchy. Yes, I even survived gay liberation (which unfortunately titles a major event Gay Games, disregarding the participation of lesbians). Nevertheless, what remains most intact and what gives me the courage to be standing here is my abiding desire to claim my place on the hill overlooking the Sheep Meadow's crest in Central Park, where the first Christopher Street Gay Pride March concluded in 1970, where as far as one could see wave upon wave of lesbians and gay men were marching to their freedom.

NOTES

1. Speech given June 25, 1994, New York University, New York, New York.

2. S.F. Dansky, "Hey Man," *RAT* Newspaper, August, 1970.

3. S.F. Dansky, John Knoebel, and Kenneth Pitchford, "The Effeminist Manifesto," *Double-F Magazine*, 1971.

4. S.F. Dansky, "Introduction." In *Now Dare Everything: Tales of HIV-Related Psychotherapy*, The Haworth Press, 1994.

Chapter 8

The Mourning Dove

For a time, while they sat together, there was an extraordinary mute passage between her vision of this vision of his, his vision of her vision, and her vision of his vision of her vision.

Henry James, *What Maisie Knew*

New York City's insistent flirtation with Indian Summer on this September morning, with temperatures into the mid-90s, intensified the pungency of melting tar, sidewalks littered with uncollected garbage, and steamy aromas escaping through fast-food air vents. I wandered lost through Washington Heights on Manhattan's Upper West Side for over half-an-hour, perplexed by the improbability of three separate streets with the same name converging into a triangular common. The apartment building, River West Terrace, overlooked the Hudson River, but the three Riverside Drives winded circularly into the distance, obscuring the river.

The sidewalks overflowed with street life, and I approached a group of Dominicans for directions while they rearranged red dominoes on a card table. Although they spoke English, no one could guide me, but fortunately an elderly Latina glanced over while simultaneously shaving ice from a large block. She poured a syrupy green liquid over the snow cone as she directed me with a wide smile, saying "No problem." Several children waited, scrutinizing me from behind the multicolored syrup bottles lining the shelf under the umbrella-shielded vendor cart.

During 1993, Washington Heights reflected the demographic evolution of New York City, becoming the volatile focus of several disquieting controversies—the common dominator of each being race. Race is fundamental to New York politics, from the philosophy of multiculturalism to sanctioning political asylum for Haitian refugees fleeing a military dictatorship. Even the Mollen Commission investigation into the New York City Police Department exposed racism, finding that the majority of crimes perpetrated by police were against people of color.

As I walked up Riverside Drive West, the sweltering heat of the streets gave way to a forceful wind, and, at last, I was confronted by the river embraced by a startling indigo sky. I realized I'd become physically out of shape as the wind pushed me backward. Hardly the personification of contemporary gay men who have taken control physically at the gym while the human immunodeficiency virus (HIV) pandemic devastates the bodies of so many others. Being a perfectionist about punctuality, I was uncomfortable about my lateness and anxious about meeting this family for the first time, hoping I would be regarded as well-meaning and unobtrusive.

There were hurdles to finding a prototypical gay family. First, there are no criteria that define the ideal family, no heritage, culture, norms, or models. Each gay parent I spoke with weighed the deep personal responsibility of protecting and preserving family normalcy against being a catalyst for political change and shouldering public attention. One gay family refused to be interviewed: their family life was disrupted for over a year by media attention. Another gay family was overextended with child-raising responsibilities and negotiating dual careers. Yet another gay parent confided that an interview with a national magazine had brought strife between himself and his partner. Surprisingly different beliefs of parenting between them emerged, which they needed to work through before being in the public limelight. As lesbian and gay parents are increasingly visible—many without fear of reprisal, some remaining vulnerable–many families are propelled into the public eye, others into court.

At the door, Stephen Curry welcomed me with a soft-spoken voice and an extended hand, and instantly, I felt relieved that I was accepted into this home. Stephen is a 38-year-old Caucasian with a well-groomed ponytail and bright hazel eyes who pointed me to the living room, saying, "Make yourself comfortable; Thieren will be with you shortly."

The foyer was lined with bookshelves on two walls, filled with books, a stereo system, several shelves of compact discs, and video-tapes. Jessye Norman's distinguished voice reverberated throughout the apartment as the heroine of Purcell's *Dido and Aeneas*, and I recognized the line "Mine with storms of care oppress'd is taught to pity the distressed." The living room was bright, with sun streaming through windows facing the river with the imposing George Washington Bridge off to the right. There were paintings on all the walls—one was African, reminiscent of Keith Haring's work, with figures randomly placed but in relation to one another, unmistakably cere-monial. Another painting was a black sharecropper couple, their middle-aged, burnt sienna-colored skin weathered by decades in the sun, between them a wide-eyed black and white calico cat.

After Stephen's hurried greeting at the door, I sat on the sofa and waited for Thieren Williamson to conclude a phone call from San Francisco. Vaulting from nowhere, Billy, their five-year-old child, leapt on the sofa next to me. He questioned, "Why are you wearing your shoes?" not exactly out of disapproval but more out of puzzle-ment. "Shouldn't I be wearing shoes?" I asked, and he replied, "We don't wear shoes in the living room." Without delay, he ques-tioned, "Why are you here?" "Do you want to see my room?" Before I could respond, he seized my hand. There were games, dolls, balls, roller skates, and toys overstuffed into plastic crates interlocked from floor to ceiling, allowing only for a bunk bed covered with wild animal sheets.

What preoccupied Billy instantly was a bird feeder outside a window. A mourning dove vacillated a few feet above the window sill, wary of the bird feeder, which had a two-way mirror permitting close observation without the silvery bird being startled. Lawrence, the nine-year-old, entered the room, informing me, "Willy's our mourning dove," before rotating on his high-top sneakers for sup-port from his father, Thieren. We went into the living room, and Thieren and Stephen sat side-by-side on a sofa with Billy's head resting on Papa's lap, and his legs extended over Daddy's. Law-rence lay on the floor fingering the pieces of another bird feeder that Thieren was assembling.

Thieren is 42 years old—an African American, originally from Chester, outside Philadelphia, where his family still lives in the house where he was raised. Thieren's two brothers and a sister reside within a ten-mile radius of his parents. Thieren, barefooted, was wearing a forest green T-shirt and dungarees, with holes stylishly at the knees. His hair was close-cropped, about the same length as his greying full beard. I was immediately impressed with his seriousness; although he expressed warmth, it was with the distinctive manner of someone insistently commanding respect, unmistakably vigilant about how people behave toward him.

Thieren studied computer science in graduate school at Ohio State University, working for NCR until the 1970s when the company offered him a position in New York City. Thieren said, "I was happy to get back to the East Coast." Currently, Thieren is a programmer for a leading banking institution. Thieren and Stephen met over ten years ago on the subway's F train, and Thieren defines their courtship as entangled. Before Stephen, Thieren had another partner for almost ten years, Edward, with whom he adopted Lawrence, the first adopted child. Once they had resolved to adopt, they were zealous about proceeding, no matter how intimidating the obstacles.

Edward was diagnosed with AIDS during the mid-1980s. When the adoption agency telephoned that they had found a boy, Lawrence, the decision facing the couple was complicated by Edward's AIDS diagnosis. If Edward's health status shifted and he became debilitated, his ability to fully participate in the rigors of childraising would be impaired. The future was uncertain, but for the time being Edward's health was stable, so the couple decided to forego long-term planning in favor of living in the present. Thieren HIV antibody-tested several times and remained HIV seronegative. Thieren said, "If both of us were HIV seropositive, we wouldn't have pursued the adoption, but Edward was adamant that we go ahead with our plans. I adopted as a single father."

Within the year Edward died. Lawrence was two years old at the time, and Thieren explained that his memory of Edward was vivid, but "children go through losses differently than adults. At two years, although Lawrence was very verbal, many feelings were not surfacing. Initially, he asked questions about Edward when he didn't return home and the hospital visits ended. I explained to him that he died and went to heaven—we couldn't see him anymore. I told Lawrence, 'Edward still loves you.'"

Thieren didn't recognize the effects of the loss on Lawrence for another year. It became evident when a close friend in Australia was dying, and Thieren visited him on a hastily planned emergency trip. Wanting to prepare Lawrence for the absence, he made audiotapes of himself reading books. When he returned home, it was very apparent how upset Lawrence was. It wasn't only Thieren's absence that upset him; feelings about Edward had surfaced. Lawrence was frightened that something would happen to Thieren. He had no idea of what that meant either in terms of illness, AIDS, or death. He just knew that Thieren was gone and Edward was gone. Though he was always available to Lawrence, Thieren had to reassure him by making himself more accessible. He canceled meetings in the evenings. He composed stories and songs about being there for Lawrence and loving him, and he talked about it a lot more. Over time, Lawrence became more comfortable.

Edward's death also affected Thieren profoundly, and although when speaking of the loss he seemed to hesitate before using the word devastating, it was catastrophic for him. For three months, Thieren had been in the stage of acute mourning, and he conceded that only Lawrence had kept him from "going over the edge." On the day Edward died, Thieren had returned from the hospital at 4:00 a.m. It was Lawrence's first day at school—he was entering a preschool program two days a week—and it was this knowledge that forced Thieren to get up when it was time and face the day. Lawrence's existence compelled him. Thieren never knew what might trigger a deep emotional reaction. He found himself crying for no reason at all while riding the subway or watching a movie. Everything evoked powerful emotions, touched him very deeply. It could have been something amusing, a detail of their life together; everything reminded him of Edward. Laughter would change to despair with tears streaming down his face. Most people describe the mourning process as similar to being in a tunnel and not seeing light for a long time. During the third month, he felt differently and his life evolved.

Thieren recalls an ostensibly seamless transition from friendship to partnership as Stephen joined the family. "Stephen and I were very close—he was Lawrence's godfather, so when Edward died it was natural and comfortable for Stephen and I to become partners—

for him to become part of our family unit. There was trust between us and it was comfortable to start a committed relationship."

On the July 4th weekend in 1988, Stephen moved in, and they started a new life. Stephen was in a Roman Catholic religious order, and his decision to be in a committed relationship with Thieren coincided with his leaving the Carmelites. Stephen asserts, "It wasn't a sudden decision for me, but I needed a booster shot. I was a chaplain at Brooklyn's Methodist Hospital and enrolled in a pastoral education program. I worked primarily with intravenous drug users (IVDUs). I had many questions about my life." Stephen was raised in upstate New York about one hour from Manhattan in a town called Cold Springs.

Thieren proceeded with adoption through two relationships: Lawrence with Edward and Billy with Stephen. They made the decision despite extraordinary obstacles. Although in New York State the law prohibits discrimination against lesbian and gay prospective adoptive parents, the implementation of the law is a different story, and the process required overcoming the prejudicial limitations of agencies and their staff. There were very few institutional exceptions.

The decision to adopt reverberated within their social support system. Some friends were supportive, others not. Most of their friends at the time were gay men. Thieren says, "I just couldn't put parenting out of my head. What catapulted me into the decision was Billy Jones, a good friend of mine, who was the former president of New York City's Health and Hospitals Corporation (HHC) under Mayor David Dinkins. He and his partner adopted a child several years previously. He was a gay parental role model: you could be gay and do it, and I met several other African Americans who've become adoptive parents."

Thieren believes that many responses to his being a parent could be seen in terms of age. His older gay friends in their fifties and sixties weren't supportive, while his peers were very supportive— many were just surprised; others saw it as revolutionary. Thieren expressed the lack of understanding from older gay men, to some degree, as internalized homophobia, stating, "The way they've survived in a society that has been so horrible to them is to set limits for their self-actualization. In a society that's been intolerant, it's difficult for them to adjust to changes despite support from the gay movement."

For people Thieren's age, the beginning of the contemporary lesbian and gay movement occurred during their adolescence and the political infrastructure developed in leaps and bounds when they were in their early twenties. Since the lesbian and gay movement became widespread during the 1970s, expanding to every major city and college campus under the *Come Out!* banner, life has changed significantly for lesbians and gay men. Older gay men, who suffered homophobia most of their adult lives, greeted the movement with mixed emotions, particularly when the early movement allied with radical political movements. The gay movement demands risk, and *coming out* is liberating, but also conveys loss—of career, family, or friends. Older gay men had principally resisted adversity through subterfuge, creating a subculture that incorporated vernacular, humor, and camp. For survival, they devised a subsystem to identify each other, establishing places to gather and sexual clandestine cruising sites. Many gay men equate acceptance of sexual identity with childlessness.

For Thieren, who had been raised in a close-knit family with strong extended family and kinship ties, children and family were an integral part of life. He always wanted to have children. Many lesbians and gay men experience the pain of *coming out*, in part, as a mourning, the loss of the experience of having children. For Thieren, acceptance of his sexual identity was foremost, and he couldn't tolerate the idea of heterosexual marriage to have children. Within our diligently homophobic culture, the segregation of gay men from children is profound. Gay men unconsciously internalize others' beliefs about their unsuitability for parenthood. Often unconsciously, gay men experience themselves as contagious, internalizing the heterosexist notion that sexual identity can be transmitted from one individual to another, despite unresolved arguments about nature versus nurture, genetics versus socialization, where sexual identity is concerned.

Thieren's eyes narrowed, and his lips widened into a grin as he described the old stories about how gay men dealt with being gay in the 1940s and 1950s. "One friend told me stories about wearing a red handkerchief on a particular day so gay men could identify themselves to each other. It was a signal for them. Their life was much more undercover. The choices we're making are radical and threatening to them."

Thieren mentioned knowing several other gay African-American males who have adopted. "Certainly, my community was African American, and I didn't have that many white friends, although there was a small group of white friends in my life. Essentially, all my friends were gay African-American males. It was a very insular community."

Thieren challenged stereotypes about the African-American experience. "The extended family is very important to us, though we've had periods, such as the last several decades, when it has been assaulted and is disintegrating." His grandparents, aunts, and uncles were omnipresent during his childhood. His oldest brother divorced early in his marriage, returning home with his three-month-old child, Derek. "We all parented Derek. I was a fifteen-year-old with specific responsibilities, but my life with my nephew was ongoing beyond daily scheduled time. By sixteen, I had a driver's license, and he went with me wherever I was going." He explained that in the African-American family, taking care of each other is very important because society has not been affirming. "We have to protect our family life."

Thieren described the gay African-American community as being wonderful and supportive when he was coming out. He described the gay African-American community as a "protective family," because in the larger black family there wasn't tolerance of difference. "The black community was accepting of gays if you weren't out of the closet: there were many who were leaders in the churches and community groups, but if you came out, that was it. You'd be ostracized. Homophobia exists in all communities." I thought of Bayard Rustin and James Baldwin and how they suffered politically and personally, never being truly accepted as gay African-American men.

In West Philadelphia where Thieren grew up gay, African-American men cultivated surrogate families. He went to an African-American college, Cheyney State University, with a gay male, and after he came out he was introduced to a group of gay African-American professionals, *Buppies*, in a sense. There was a party given for him, and many of the people at the party became big brothers—mentors—to him. I thought of the film *Paris Is Burning*, which was about the phenomenon of so-called *houses*, virtually unknown to the Caucasian gay male community. Houses are a form of communal living arrangement by transgenderists, observing a strict hierarchy under the leadership of a main individual by which the house is named. The film is a cinéma vérité depiction of drag balls—in which black and Latino men don *vogueing* disguises from flamboyant gowns to coat-and-tie conservative businessmen attire. The house is a form of brotherhood that requires total loyalty and is structured to provide an alternate family system.

Thieren thinks men are becoming more visible as parents. "I see men in nursery schools as parents, as well as professionals in early childhood education. When I was growing up, fathers weren't supposed to see their child in kindergarten—it was a woman's responsibility. What it says to me as a man is that I'm allowed, that I permit myself, to express an aspect of my nature that has always been there, nurturing. I can express affection to my children, tell them that I love them, be present for the crises, and happy moments."

The family weathered the political upheaval surrounding the rainbow curriculum through involvement from the beginning of the controversy. Thieren said, "Our family was the first family on national television to discuss the rainbow curriculum. We appeared on Ted Koppel's Nightline. It aired the day school opened last year. We're activists because education is paramount to our children's lives. The irony about the controversy is that the lesbian and gay parent issue became the entire focus of debate." Thieren asserts, "My children will most likely be heterosexual—I believe in the 10 percent figure. They'll be invited to communities we have been denied access, and they'll share their experience of being raised by two gay fathers."

Unfortunately, many in the lesbian and gay community don't understand why they should be supportive of children. Thieren recalled, "When we go to a gay restaurant, for instance, we're considered a nuisance because we have children with us. I remember an AIDS Committee to Unleash Power (ACT UP) meeting where a woman had her children with her, and she was asked to leave because her children were making noise. That is not unusual

because many organizations in the gay male community don't provide day care spaces. The assumption is that we don't have children. Women have been much more conscious about this issue—men
have a lot to work through."

Everything in Thieren's and Stephen's lives has completely
changed because of parenting. When Thieren first adopted Lawrence, he arrived on a Friday, and the following Monday, Thieren
missed the opera, *X*—the opera about Malcolm X; he's an ardent
opera lover. Someone could have baby-sat for a couple of hours, but
he didn't want to leave his newly adopted child.

The direction of his life began to shift. He couldn't spontaneously
go out to dinner without his baby, saying "When they're infants you
don't want to leave them. Our lives to this day revolve around our
children. For instance, yesterday there was a soccer tournament in
the morning, and in the afternoon, there was a Center Kids picnic in
Central Park." Thieren recalled, "Last year when Lawrence rode his
bicycle for the first time, a two-wheeler, it was a major accomplishment. We rejoiced. When Billy went to his first Radio City Music
Hall Christmas Show, and he saw Santa Claus rise into the air, he
was so incredibly shocked that his mouth just dropped. We were
together for all major events, such as his first Halloween party."

The decision to adopt has implications beyond their circle of
lesbian and gay friends, and Thieren describes being very active in
their children's lives, ensuring that they have a protected life. "I
draw on my experience growing up African American in a white
supremacist society. Growing up in the 1950s meant that my parents were vigilant about their children—they made certain that we
were safe and protected. We lived in a safe neighborhood and were
involved in supportive institutions, such as the black church. We do
the same things for our children. We live in this community. Our
neighbors in this building have been very supportive."

Thieren explained, "Today, we're moving, although lesbian and
gay parents are not completely accepted, but we're moving." Thier-
en credits Center Kids, of which he was a former co-chairperson, as
a source of political advocacy for lesbian and gay parents and as a
support network. "In 1985, when I first began this process, none of
this was happening. There wasn't a Center Kids, and I only knew a
handful of gay people who adopted children." Thieren speculated

that younger gay male activists do not focus on the day-to-day rigors of parenting, but instead think of adoption as radical chic, another radical thing to do. "Although I want to avoid generalizations–they're all not like that."

Thieren says, "Tomorrow, I am speaking at a conference before all the executive directors of each adoption agency in New York City, which is an extraordinary accomplishment for our movement compared to the 1980s." The conference is cosponsored by New York City's Child Welfare Administration (CWA) and Center Kids. "Center Kids is the most important support system we have. Through the organization we've met other lesbian and gay families. It's important for them to know we're not the only family with two daddies or two mommies." With the pride of accomplishment, Thieren let me know that the Commissioner of CWA will attend, and he mandated that all executive directors attend the event so they will be prepared to provide services to prospective lesbian and gay parents.

The selection of appropriate schools was carefully deliberated. Lawrence attends a school for gifted children, and Billy will be starting kindergarten. The principal was told that Lawrence's parents were gay, and Thieren and Stephen spoke to the president of the Parent-Teacher Association (PTA). They explored whether the school would be a comfortable environment for their family. On open school day, when the parents and teachers meet, Thieren and Stephen disclosed that they were a gay family. It was not for political advantage, but in anticipation of questions that, no doubt, will be asked of their children. "We explained that Lawrence and Billy have two daddies. We intend to ensure that there is support and understanding for our children. We also want our children to receive a positive message from us as openly gay parents–it's integral to developing self-esteem so they're secure adults."

Thieren and Stephen acknowledge the hours are long and stressful–they're hands-on parents. We have been sitting together for hours, and the children have become restless. Lawrence calls Thieren "Daddy," and Stephen "Papa." He turns to Stephen saying "Papa, I'm hungry." It is the seemingly simple messages and natural statements such as this that make it clear that a child perceives *this* as his family.

Chapter 9

The Natural History
of Affection Between Males

> How enormous the frustration, disappointment, and despair of
> the child are at moments of utter, unrelieved defeat can be seen
> from his temper tantrums, which are the visible expression of
> the conviction that he can do nothing to improve the "unbear-
> able" conditions of his life.

> Bruno Bettelheim, *The Uses of Enchantment*

Several months had passed since the last visit and negotiations
continued between myself and the two daddies. Penetrating into the
life of this family evoked feelings of apprehension in me, which I
interpreted as my need for self-protection and fear of vulnerability as
the life of the family insinuated itself into my own. Simultaneously, I
knew the only worthy story required a commitment of several years of
intimacy and involvement. Maintaining distance would be contradictory to what I believed would be the relevancy of the book. A true
understanding of this extraordinary family would be compromised if I
imposed constraints from a need to be self-contained or uninvolved.
The self-revelation came after months of questioning my own tenta-
tiveness. The family was guarded, but welcoming, weary of being in
public view, but accessible. It was my projection to represent the
family as defended against intrusion—caution was a subterfuge so that I
could be untouched by their power. The family embodied spirit and
vitality, and I did not want to be emotionally moved or have memories
of my childhood deprivation reactivated. So even though writers are
thought to merely make a case, illuminating darkness with a lightning
flash, challenging the gods—that is, values—then moving on, something

different was happening to me. This family was in the public and
political arena, making history, but it was their individual sensibilities
and the significance of family that I wanted the book to convey; I
wanted to free the reader's imagination to behold the precious reality
of this family.

During a dinner visit with the family, we devoured a pizza, with
Lawrence and Billy looking on as Thieren, Stephen, and I disputed the
nature of political evolution. It was evident that each of us was propelled by the urgency of our lives. Stephen asked, "Did you see the
Jonathan Demme film *Philadelphia?*" I answered, "Yes." Thieren
said, "The dilemma for me is the film's apoliticism. There's no persua-
sive argument to counterpoint the all-too-familiar and recognizable
homophobia of the lawyer, portrayed by Denzel Washington. His homophobia is socially familiar and unchallenged except on a personal
level." Thieren was indicating that justice is not solely an appeal for a
humanistic understanding of diversity, but that social change demands
political context, structure, and theory. As he asserted, "We can't rely
on people's good nature."

Surely in *Philadelphia* it is only when the lawyer witnesses the
person with AIDS (PWA), portrayed by Tom Hanks, rhythmically
moving to the strains of Maria Callas singing the aria, *La Mamma
Morta* from the opera *Andrea Chenier*, as he Christ-like clutched an
intravenous pole, that his homophobia transforms into compassion,
and he admires the courage of the gay man. There is a persistent
demand that the lawyer, played by Washington, behold the PWA's
humanity as a gay man, suffer with him, and tolerate his pain as a
fellow human being. Ultimately, the lawyer flees the apartment, returning to the familiarity of his life. He had observed the illumination
of the body electric. It was not a hallucination, and the PWA's mag-
netism must be accommodated into his experience.

Lesbians and gay men have been stereotyped as victims, either
scolded or pitied. Our way of life, of love, has been a secret to
humanity. Homophobia is psychological pathology–a compulsion to
deny reality that is born out of fear. Individuals are not afraid of
something that does not exist. Science will change in time, and there
are theories that cannot be worked out in a laboratory. In this century,
the genetic association to sexual identity is merely an idea.

Thieren and Stephen each maintained, "There's nothing unusual about our family. What will you write about? Nothing happens." I argued to Thieren and Stephen, "Nothing happens? Nothing happens by political force alone without the transformation of human spirit. We have relied on legislation and law, but synchronous with systemic change must be an alteration of consciousness, which takes decades. No, centuries."

We were interrupted by the telephone ringing. It was a gay organization requesting to photograph the family for display on a T-shirt. Thieren shrugged his shoulders, uncertain that he'd want to appear on merchandise. The family would be emblematic, through a singular statement, a reductionist message of consumerism: "We exist." Herein lies the paradox for the family–their attempt to preserve their essence and privacy against their ambitious passion to filter their experience into the lesbian and gay community and into society. The children needed to be bathed and put to bed, and we planned for me to spend Sunday with Lawrence and Billy.

The demands of the day were anticipated because Thieren and Stephen sufficiently warned me that the children would incite power struggles and test the limits of my authority. I assured them with overconfident bravado, "I'm not new to children, and I'm certainly not new to power struggles." On Saturday, I lounged more than usual, took a lavish bubble bath, and fell asleep with headphones on, listening to the mesmerizing chant of the singing quartet, Anonymous 4. They paid homage to the female principle and goddess-worship, harmonizing a medieval polyphony to the Virgin Mary. Outside, an unrelenting snowfall pummeled New York with excessive force, nearly setting a record for the century.

I awakened to the predawn haze feeling emotionally intoxicated, as if the world were possessed by eroticism, violence, and implausibility. It was the day before St. Valentine's, and I scribbled images that seemed to have mythic significance into a dream book. After a fitful sleep I was impressed that even the force of absolute will has no dominion over the extravagances of the subconscious. My conscious mind would have censored any wish-fulfillment dreamscape.

I reached the West Side early enough to stop at a coffee bar for a third cup of coffee–chocolate mint cappuccino. The pewter landscape of winter contradicted my tenacious longing and the sensuality of the previous night's dreams, silencing my protests against single life. The city streets were abandoned; even the homeless fled their cardboard box shelters in pursuit of warmth, joining the mole people in the subway underground.

Cars parked along Riverside Drive were scarcely visible; several broke down to languish in the road, their windshields covered with snow. On this Sunday morning, the freezing rain varnished the streets, and sharply reflecting ice patches were more than an inconvenience even with the traction of heavy construction boots. Vaporous fog submerged the New Jersey horizon, transmuting the shoreline into an opaque smudge indistinguishable from the river water. Fragmented ice floes dotted the Hudson River, moving toward the bay in randomly transforming patterns.

The hallway vestibule to the apartment was lined with rows of soaked-through shoes, and several pairs of snow boots dried with Pollock-esque patterns created by rock salt. I leaned against the wall to remove my waterlogged boots. I lightly knocked, interrupting the absolutely silent Sunday morning. Billy inspected me from behind the slightly ajar front door, and without any words or gestures closed the door in my face. He seemed entertained by the game, but I intuited some other meaning. The opening-and-closing door game suggested Billy's ambivalence, his experimenting with the boundaries of inner safety against the uncertainty of the external world. During my initial visit, Billy cross-examined the purpose of my visit while leaping into my lap. This conflict intimates a discrepancy between feelings and behavior. He seemed to exhibit feelings of skepticism and guardedness, but behaved impulsively by bouncing into my lap.

The issue of trust versus mistrust is resolved during the first year of infancy. Trust is a primary function of the development of ego, and must be initiated and nurtured through sensitive, consistent, and trustworthy caregiving. When there is early abandonment, lack of continuity, and inadequate attention, or in severe instances, traumata, the normal crisis of separation from the caregiver becomes unsuccessful with symptoms of mistrust reoccurring in various ways throughout childhood. All children must resolve separation anxiety, which can be dominated by rage and temper tantrums. When the caregiver abandons the child or if boundaries are inconsistent for a child whose parents are present, anxiety and uncertainty will manifest in the adult through a mistrustful personality fluctuating between overdependent demands on and indifferent remoteness to others.

Billy's hesitation to admit me through the door into the circumference of his home was being resolved through a ritualistic, symbolic game, denoting the ambivalence of interrelationships for him. Billy ran past me into the living room, whimsically tumbling to the floor in a playact fall. The apartment was hushed until Lawrence whizzed into the room on a two-wheeled bike. Both children retreated to their rooms, changing from pajamas to street clothing.

I waited alone in the living room, a spectator to every gesture and each movement, as if everything contained a distinct meaning to which I could apply language. I experienced myself as a psychological device, suspended in midair, orbiting the panorama of this family. It was comparable to my habitual interpretation of content hidden beneath the surface of language and bodily movements during a psychotherapeutic session. It was as if I had come from another country to observe this room. The textures of the apartment were palpable as I waited alone. I reexperienced the room, transforming paintings and objects into sensations of pain, struggle, and joy, rather than mere prototypes of a multicultural commitment.

The laundry lay in piles on the sofa, a folded T-shirt revealed the insignia of the 1993 Gay and Lesbian March on Washington. Thieren appeared, hurriedly getting Lawrence and Billy ready for Sunday school, brushing Billy's hair and at the same time wiping Lawrence's nose. Thieren wore a skin-tight gray turtleneck, tucking it into his jeans while smoothing wrinkles that might interfere with the contour of his buttocks. He conducted himself with deliberate precision and attentiveness to the details of appearance. My first response at noticing the trait was probably homophobic, interpreting the gesture as narcissistic. But I recognized the care extended to the children as he fingered Billy's hair, saying, "You're getting a haircut tonight." Billy replied with concise rebellion, "No I'm not." Billy's will to assert himself, his need to have his way, was a forewarning of the afternoon. He was simultaneously depending on the caregiver and struggling for control and autonomy.

The car ride took less than ten minutes, but getting the children fastened in their safety belts was a tedious maneuver. When Thieren closed the car door, Lawrence moaned, "You shut it on my nose," and it suggested another ritualistic diversion, one of Lawrence's tactics to draw attention to his oppositional nature.

The imposing spires of Riverside Church came into view, effortlessly reigning over the West Side. The strange beauty and power of French Gothic medievalism seems anachronistic in modern New York with the limestone facade overlooking some of the most wretched of neighborhoods, rising above the noisiest of traffic. The church is an imposing symbol of supreme authority. The children attended separate Sunday school classes and weren't going to the church service. Stephen left Thieren and me to go set up a room for a symposium on homophobia in the Bible, sponsored by the lesbian and gay church group. For a millisecond it seemed an earlier period, as I recalled decades of gay liberation workshops. I felt fatigued by the struggle to be understood. It was like trying to assert oneself in a straitjacket.

The grandeur of the nave was impressive with its thrilling piers springing almost a hundred feet high to a vaulted ceiling. Thieren remarked, "Usually, the church is filled. I guess the weather kept people home." The congregation represented an Upper West Side community cross section—those who appeared to be academicians from nearby Columbia University, others working class, clusters of lesbians and gay men, and African Americans, many of whom were wearing the geometric motifs of the Ashanti, Masai, and Bariba. Riverside was responsive historically to political progressiveness, cultural and sexual diversity, and the needs of the community. I thought of its decades of social consciousness, and its activism against the Vietnam War, providing sanction to antiwar dissenters.

The pastor, Dr. Forbes, announced *love* was the sermon topic, and I chafed in the wooden pew anticipating a succession of clichés. Forbes' oratory style was self-assured, and his voice penetrated the space despite his rasping due to a cold. Thieren told me that approximately one-third of the congregation is lesbian and gay, and Forbes supported them during the sermon by referring several times to the bonding vows of domestic partnership. He defined love between partners as the friction, wearing away, and transformation of each by the other. He portrayed love as risk, the consummate uncertainty, a stretching beyond self through commitment, without knowing the consequences, suggestive of Scott Peck's assertion, "Love is volitional rather than emotional." Love is not a feeling.

During the sermon, I experienced the intensity of Thieren's receptivity as he nodded in affirmation or expressed assent with an intermittent "Uh huh" or "Yes." I thought of Thieren's struggle against militancy and rage against social injustice tempered by love for his partner and children. It must be an emotional tug-of-war between obedience and rebellion. He undeniably knows too much of two segregated societies, and he lives at the intersection of each, performing a brilliant balancing act.

I recalled a photograph of Thieren that was sitting on top of the piano in their living room. He was in his twenties with a sweater ivy-leaguishly draped over his shoulders. He clearly made something of a splash in his youth—the rest of his life ripples out from the handsome image. His sensuality is undefeated, he hasn't surrendered without a struggle, but there is devastation in his eyes, as if something were devouring his heart. I tried to imagine what he felt during the sermon. Was he thinking of Stephen, Lawrence, and Billy? Or something more existential—the core of self-esteem and a yearning for freedom? He must have sensed what I was thinking as he turned to me asking, "Do you have a partner?" I replied defensively, "It's been years."

The sermon concluded and Thieren sank into the pew as if the years of his middle life had restrained the blazing sexual fireworks of the period of coming out (which he previously described to me), when the momentum of choice was erotically induced by physical attraction to the exclusion of knowing the person holistically, that is, mentally, physically, and spiritually. The gross hazards of eroticism were more dangerous than ever with the HIV retrovirus baffling science. But, *it* was always dangerous. Before the epidemic, my next-door neighbor was murdered as he lay in bed by a man he met in a gay bar. The police interviewed me the next day, and said the multiple stab wounds were savage. Surely, one might argue being murdered while having sex is considered rarer than dying of HIV disease, but how many gay men have risked their lives, been incarcerated, dishonorably discharged from the military, banned from their family, or committed suicide in pursuit of a sexual life?

The voice of angels within the cathedral undermined sexual materialism by instilling the congregation with the conceptualization of a superior love. My blood was charged with yearning, but paradise lost is not regained through sex. We left the sanctuary to collect Lawrence and Billy for our day's excursion. The school's new director greeted Thieren. Immediately, he disclosed the composition of the family, and without hesitation, her moon face impassive, she embraced the information. They spoke for a few minutes and shook hands vigorously.

Lawrence and Billy went to the bathroom and kissed Daddy and Papa goodbye. It was early afternoon, but the sky had darkened ominously as we approached a curb on Claremont Avenue. The sewer drainage was backed up, producing a glacial soup of half-melted ice. Almost predictably, Lawrence and Billy deliberated with confidence, then plunged ankle-deep into the lake. We walked toward a bus stop, Lawrence leading a few feet ahead, and Billy holding my hand. We boarded a bus, deciding to purchase movie tickets for the latest Disney film, which they had already seen, but wanted to see again.

The initial challenge came from Billy a block from the movie theater as he was tempted by the sight of a purple-and-white mechanical horse outside a toy store. He demanded, "I want to ride the horse." There was a silent interval as Billy and I became two opposing camps. I became aware of the dangers and limitations of any relationship when conflict occurs and there is no history to draw upon, no frame of reference. We'd never be able to mediate what was about to happen, certainly not within a linguistic context. If I expressed the last word, simply "no," there would be little chance for any positive outcome.

For a while our eyes were held by the display of falling snow, particles doing everything acrobatically possible—the bigger flakes suggested the astral storming of one of Van Gogh's night skies. I said, "We have a lot to do, so we can't stop for you to ride the horse." The plumpness of Billy's dimpled cheeks became rigid, making the bones of his skull prominent—the enchantment of his eyes was obscured by insurgency. He couldn't help himself. The rest followed from this.

Billy dismissed me as I offered my hand crossing the street, and I recognized that the power struggle had escalated to another level. We reached McDonald's without incident, but Billy lingered defiantly behind. When I turned to the clerk to order—Lawrence asked for a children's special that included a toy—with my back turned, in a flash, Billy punched Lawrence. Lawrence returned with a hit to Billy's face. The two children were fighting in the middle of the food order. The clerk registered her displeasure because the purchase was interrupted by administering to the children. The long line of patrons began rumbling as they were detained.

It was total pandemonium at McDonald's. A Caucasian with two African-American children does not go unnoticed, and the patrons scrutinized me as if I were an extraterrestrial as I tried my damnedest to be relaxed. For survival, I decided to block everyone out because all the patrons' eyes seemed to be on me. I imagined they judged my inability to quiet Billy, whose outcries shook his entire body. I had no option but to block everything from view.

Billy's temper tantrum was relentless. He refused to eat his meal, holding his eye, saying, "It hurts." Clearly displeased, Lawrence ate his burger in silence. The crying continued despite efforts by another clerk who brought two balloons to the table. Billy refused his and Lawrence held the string of the other one expressionlessly.

Then, I thought, they must think I've harmed him. Then, "What's this white guy doing with two black kids." Then, "This guy's some faggot who's kidnapped two kids." Feeling totally incompetent, I momentarily diverted my frustration with the fantasy of standing on a table to plead my case and proclaim my innocence. "You see, it's not my fault. I was just ordering a kid's meal. . . . And . . . I'm not hurting these black children. Well, I'm a friend. I know you don't believe that, but. . . ." The only viable strategy was to block everything out of view. Demoralized, I nervously ate the cold burger while Billy's weeping oscillated between whimpering and rage.

I decided to cancel the movie plan and take them home. Billy refused to walk so I thought, "Who cares?" and I carried him out to the street, fumbling in my pockets for a quarter to telephone his parents. I couldn't manage holding Billy and dialing, so I put him down to discover an out-of-order phone. We walked for several blocks, finally finding another phone only to discover there was no answer at their home.

I hailed a gypsy cab and sped uptown, emotionally confused, feeling lackluster and inadequate with the all-too-common, tearing-at-the-gut sensation of self-questioning. It became externalized into the exclamation: "Why do I live in New York?" Billy fell asleep, consumed by the tantrum, his body inclined against my lap. The imprint of tears dried translucently on his cheek, and the diminutive clenched fist that masked his eyes dropped into his lap. Lawrence appeared hurt during the silent trip, and I rubbed his back, a small comfort, as he watched passing traffic.

I carried Billy, still asleep, into the building, and the doorman said that Thieren and Stephen had not returned home, and offered us the key to the community room. Once inside the community room, Billy awakened as if nothing had happened, climbing the steps of a slide. Lawrence zoomed past me on a bicycle, crashing into a large plywood dollhouse. Billy's eyes widened as if to say, "Let's go," and with a celebratory scream of joy he tumbled down the slide, while I observed with a dazed stare.

Lawrence took the toy from McDonald's from his pocket and showed it to Billy, who exclaimed, "Where's mine?" I gave the toy to him and deposited myself on a bench by the mahogany upright piano. Lawrence sat with me, placing his elegant fingers on the yellowed keys and began playing a few bars of the Duke Ellington jazz classic "*A* Train," which he was practicing for a school talent recital. It was safe here: Billy was swept away by the tantrum and had calmed down, totally spent. I knew that Billy had been experiencing an intolerable helplessness deflating any previous sense of magical omnipotence.

They played with ferocious, kinetic energy for an hour until Thieren and Stephen returned home, encountering in the community room a scene that misrepresented the chaotic afternoon. Lawrence and Billy were beyond the small drama and embraced their daddies as I stretched vertically along a slide, completely drained and self-consciously defeated. With reluctance, I reported some of the afternoon's events to the parents' dismay, and Stephen demanded apologies from the children both to each other and to me. Billy groped for the language, although words were useless except for an apology to Lawrence and me. His small fingers covered his face and his cries became mewing whimpers. Lawrence expressed anger and had to be encouraged to talk.

I was relieved once the visit was over, and returned home to reconstitute and organize the experience. The intensity of sibling rivalry is similar to momentary madness, a form of possession, and in half a minute well-mannered children can transform calm into fury. After recovering from the baffling humiliation of the day, I realized my Promethean self-confidence had interfered with thoughtful planning. I had expected benevolence and goodwill to suffice without having considered the changed emotional rhythm and the alteration of the children's familiar space.

Most children dream of being independent or of having other parents more powerful and more perfect than their own. But adopted children, whose destiny is shaped by the actual loss of one or both parents, dream of their own survival and fear being responsible for either their parents' death or the dissolution of the family of origin. Everyone undergoes losses that determine the passages and benchmarks of development. While being weaned, infants slowly become conscious that they are different entities from the caregiver. They become aware of limits, both of their body and self, separate from the caregiver. The differentiation is complex, and active resistance to the authority of adults is part of the process. In disrupted families in which nurturing is inconsistent and object constancy is lacking, children experience developmental challenges when the too-sudden and painful realization of their helplessness becomes intensified by authentic abandonment.

Billy evoked the archetype of an abandoned child confronted by a life of *mythical dangers*, causing him to live through an agony of panic, fears, and terrors of all kinds. Along with his fear and anxiety that the caregiver would disappear, and in an attempt to defend himself from it, he displayed the need for a pseudo-independence and a panicky anxiety at allowing me too close to him emotionally. The so-called *good* child was superficially compliant, and the so-called *bad* child resisted me in his life. When his attempts to control me were frustrated, he lost control of himself, bringing forth a powerful need for revenge. The temper tantrum expressed his being unable to have me, so I could not have him.

Orphans and adopted children experience more intensely than others the fundamental human experience of separation from the caregiver. The most painful losses are those relating to ideals that give a sense of order to one's life, because their loss calls into question the individual's self-identity. The loss of one or both parents provokes a crisis that imposes new adjustments, in particular with regard to the internal changes such a rupture demands of a relationship.

It was critical to my relationship with Lawrence and Billy to provide further opportunities for them to experience security and protection with me. The chance came during the following week when Thieren telephoned to invite me to a talent show sponsored by the Black Parents Association at Lawrence's elementary school.

It was an astonishingly bright Sunday afternoon. I luxuriated in the sunshine for a few minutes before entering the school. I recognized Billy playing at the entrance to the auditorium, but he disappeared into a corridor, and I waited for him to come back. Clearly, there was a residual effect of our day together, an undercurrent of feeling toward me, as he acknowledged me with reticence. He nodded a greeting and painstakingly walked backwards away from me. Internally, I resisted any inclination to exaggerate, minimize, or ignore his response although I felt rejected, almost apologetic for being present.

Thieren and Stephen were in the auditorium assisting the talent show setup. They are involved parents who unfalteringly extend their commitment from the family to the community. The unity of their family is palpable and every opportunity to be present in the world is unselfconsciously seized. Stephen was on the stage making adjustments to the set, and Thieren was taping a microphone to a baby grand piano. Lawrence ran up the center aisle toward me and leapt into my arms, and Thieren noted with surprise, "I guess he's glad to see you." It was touching and flooded me with an awareness, an inner desire for connection to a child.

The talent show took endless hours, but my attention was unqualified; anything less would have been a disloyalty. The program contained a four-children tumbling act to the theme song from *Aladdin*; a rendition of Hanon's piano finger exercises; and an eight-year-old girl almost paralyzed with stage fright, ironically singing Bette Midler's sentimental "Wind Beneath My Wings" with her arms stiffly held to her torso and her hands tightly clenched.

After an intermission, Lawrence took his place at the piano, and the melody of "*A* Train" "kicked like crazy" (one of Ellington's phrases) the meaning of classical, displacing Mozart's "Twinkle, Twinkle" at this moment in history. Lawrence returned to his seat after playing and was instantaneously joined by Billy. Billy gently nuzzled his head to rest against his brother's chest, challenging the myth that men can't bond in a committed, nonoppressive loving relationship—there is a natural history of the affection between males.

Chapter 10

The First Time, the Only Time, Each Time

In the middle-class United States, a veneer of *alternative life-styles* disguises the reality that, here as everywhere, women's apparent *choices* whether or not to have children are still dependent on the far from neutral will of male legislators, jurists, a male medical and pharmaceutical profession, well-financed lobbies, including the prelates of the Catholic Church, and the political reality that women do not as yet have self-determination over our bodies and still live mostly in ignorance of our authentic physicality, our possible choices, our eroticism itself.

Adrienne Rich,
"Motherhood: The Contemporary Emergency
and the Quantum Leap," paper, June 2, 1978,
read at Future of Mothering Conference,
Columbus, OH

The fact that nearly 70 percent of HIV disease cases among women are drug-related coupled with the rapid rise of HIV infection among women makes it imperative to address the issue of substance use in women. Reliable epidemiological data on the nature and extent of drug abuse among women is needed, including data on the prevalence and use among different groups of minority women and among women of different sexual orientations. Among the many factors in the etiology of drug use among women are childhood and adolescent sexual victimization, partner violence, and anxiety disorders and depression. Certain psychological disorders are more prevalent among women than men, and women are often inappropriately prescribed medications for the treatment of anxiety and affective disorders, resulting in the overprescription and abuse of psychotherapeutic medications. There may be biological and behavioral mechanisms that clarify women's patterns of substance use. There are also differences in how drugs affect men and women: for example, animal and human studies suggest a potential connection between the menstrual cycle of substance-addicted women and drug-seeking behavior. Substance use prevention and treatment interventions for girls and women need to respond to specific gender-based risk factors, such as childhood sexual abuse and partner violence.

Epidemiological data of alcohol drinking patterns in the United States suggest that men are more likely to drink alcohol, drink heavily, and have more legal and psychosocial problems related to alcohol consumption compared to women. The biological basis for these gender differences in problem drinking is unknown. It is possible that there are gender differences in either vulnerability to the reinforcing effects of ethanol or sensitivity to the behavioral effects of ethanol. Although some studies suggest that the consumption of alcohol is influenced by the menstrual cycle, the relationship between reproductive function and alcohol is difficult to study in humans for ethical, logistical, and financial reasons. Behavioral responses to alcohol are difficult to study because the expectations of those who drink about the effects of alcohol strongly influence their social and affective behavior after drinking.

There is a high proportion of cocaine use among Caucasian and African-American female homicide victims, which appears to contradict surveys that suggest women are less likely than men to be substance users and shows that drug use is a key risk factor for homicide victimization among women. See Figure 10.1 for the connection between homicide and cocaine; Figure 10.2 for victims of homicide; Figure 10.3 for female cocaine use in homicide victims; and Figure 10.4 for female substance use. Female cocaine users are more likely than nonusers to be victims of violence from spouses, boyfriends, or, in the case of prostitutes, their clients.[1] The high homicide rate among African Americans and Latinos can be attributed to the increased availability and abuse of crack cocaine and the increased availability and lethal firepower of guns. Current

FIGURE 10.1. Cocaine and Homicide

- Nearly 3 out of every 10 homicide victims in New York City in the early 1990s had evidence of cocaine in their bodies when they died.

- Overall, murder victims in the city are 10 to 50 times more likely than members of the general population to be cocaine users, depending on age, race, and gender, according to NIDA-funded research using data from the New York City medical examiner.

- About three-fourths of all the murders involved firearms.

- Cocaine was found in 31 percent of the 4,298 people murdered in New York City in 1990 and 1991.

Source: Tardiff et al., "Homicide in New York City," 1994.

FIGURE 10.2. Homicide Victims

- Young African-American and Latino men were more likely to be victims of homicide than were members of all other demographic groups.

- Two-thirds of the victims were between the ages of 15 and 34, 86 percent were male, and 87 percent were African American or Latino.

- The rate of homicide was highest for African-American males ages 15 to 24, followed by African-American males ages 25 to 34.

- The next highest homicide rates were among young Latino men ages 25 to 34 and 15 to 24, respectively.

- African-American women and Latino women had much lower rates of death by homicide than their male counterparts.

- However, their rates were slightly higher than those of white males, particularly in the 15- to 34-year-old age group.

- White females had the lowest homicide rates of any demographic group.

Source: NIDA Notes (National Institute on Drug Abuse), March/April 1995.

FIGURE 10.3. Female Cocaine Use in Homicide Victims

- 59 percent of white women and 72 percent of African-American women ages 25 to 34 had been using cocaine before they died, compared with
- 38 percent of white men and 44 percent of African-American men in that age group.

Source: Tardiff et al., "Homicide in New York City," 1994.

FIGURE 10.4. Women and Substance Use

- Almost half of all women in their childbearing years, ages 15 to 44, have used illicit drugs at least once in their lives.
- 10.3 million women age 12 and older have used at least one illegal drug in the past year.
- More than 4.4 million women age 12 and older currently use illegal drugs.
- 4 million women have taken prescription drugs nonmedically during the past year.
- An estimated 221,000 women who gave birth in the United States in 1992 used illicit drugs while they were pregnant.
- More than 34,000—about 67 percent—of the AIDS cases among women are drug related.

Source: NIDA Notes, January/February 1995.

research is examining the connection between drug use and a broad range of crimes, including homicide, rape, domestic violence, child abuse, and gang-related violence. A team of researchers studying 4,298 homicides in New York City during 1990 and 1991 discovered that 31 percent of the victims had cocaine in their bodies. Surprisingly, among some of the young demographic groups of victims, cocaine use was higher among females than males.

Drug dependence is a combination of psychological and physical conditions characterized by a compulsion to take a substance to experience its psychological effects. Addiction is a severe form of dependence, marked by physical and psychological dependence. The latter state exists when the drug has produced physiological changes in the body, evidenced by the development of tolerance, so that increasing amounts of the drug are needed to achieve the same effect, and of a withdrawal syndrome after the drug's effects have worn off. See Figure 10.5 for symptoms of drug withdrawal syndrome.

Scientists often measure a drug's potential for abuse through studies with laboratory animals. Drugs that an animal will administer to itself repeatedly are said to have powerful reinforcing properties and a high potential for abuse. Examples include some of the major abused drugs–opium, alcohol, cocaine, and barbiturates. Other drugs, such as marijuana and the hallucinogens, appear to produce habituation in humans, even though they are not powerful reinforcers for laboratory animals. Isolated substances called enkephalins, which are naturally occurring opiates in the brain, may account for physical dependence on opioids–that is, the drugs are thought to mimic the action of enkephalins. If true, this hypothesis suggests that physical dependence on the opioids may develop in persons who have a deficiency in these natural substances. Drug use for nonmedical purposes occurs throughout society. See Figure 10.6 for the prevalence of substance use in the United States.

The number of illicit drug users has not changed since 1992. See Figure 10.7 for substance use trends. This follows more than a decade of decline since the peak year for illicit drug use, which was 1979. No change in the number of weekly cocaine users has been detected since the survey first estimated this in 1985, indicating a continuing demand for drug abuse treatment services. However, the number of occasional cocaine users has declined dramatically. The

FIGURE 10.5. Symptoms of Drug Withdrawal Syndrome

• Diarrhea	• Sweating
• Nausea	• Cramps
• Pain	• Fever
• Kicking movements in the legs	• Vomiting
• Insomnia	• Anxiety

FIGURE 10.6. U.S. Prevalence of Substance Use

- More than two-thirds of young adults (ages 18 to 25) reported experience with an illicit substance.
- Slightly less than 1 in 3 had used marijuana.
- About 1 in 5 had used hallucinogens.
- More than 1 in 4 had used cocaine.
- 1.1 percent had used heroin. (Use of heroin tends to be underestimated by household surveys because they miss, for example, the prison population.)
- Among older adults, more than 1 in 5 reported having used marijuana.
- More than 1 in 20 had used hallucinogens.
- Nearly 1 in 10 had used cocaine.
- And 1 in 100 had used heroin.
- 13 million Americans (6.0 percent of those 12 years old and older) used illicit drugs.
- 10 million Americans (four-fifths of current illicit drug users) used marijuana, making it the most commonly used illicit drug.
- 1.4 million Americans (0.7 percent of the population) used cocaine.
- 13 million Americans (6.2 percent of the population) had five or more drinks per occasion on five or more days in the month.
- 60 million people, including 4 million adolescents ages 12 to 17, smoked cigarettes.

Source: NIDA, Household Survey, 1982.

rate of past-month alcohol use declined from 1979 to 1992. Since then, the rate has increased slightly. The rate of heavy alcohol use has not changed since 1990.

Many women of childbearing age who use substances reduce substance use during pregnancy, but resume use after giving birth. This finding supports efforts to intervene with pregnant substance-users. Illicit drug use rates remain highly correlated with employment status. The highest rate of drug use was among the unemployed. However, three-quarters of adult illicit drug users and 65 percent of adult cocaine users were employed. Among persons 18 to 34 years old, those who had not completed high school had the

FIGURE 10.7. Substance Use Trends

- Between 1992 and 1994, the rate of marijuana use among youths 12 to 17 years old nearly doubled. Adolescent use had declined from 1979 to 1992.
- Since 1992, the percentage of youths 12 to 17 years old that believe there is great risk of harm in using marijuana occasionally has decreased. This points out the need for prevention efforts directed toward children and adolescents.
- There has been a shift in the age distribution of illicit drug users. The heavy drug using cohorts of the 1970s, including those with severe problems, continue to get older.
- The average age of current illicit drug users and the proportion that are age 35 and older have risen steadily since 1979.
- In 1994, the rate of current illicit drug use was highest among persons 18 to 21 and 16 to 17 years old.
- Heavy drinking was most prevalent among persons ages 18 to 21 and 22 to 25.

highest rates of illicit drug use. However, three-quarters of illicit drug users and 63 percent of cocaine users in this age group were high school graduates.

Pregnant women and other women of childbearing age are equally likely to have used licit and illicit substances at some time in their lives. Among all women ages 15 to 44, 47 percent have at some time used illicit drugs, compared with 46 percent among currently pregnant women. Rates of past year alcohol and cigarette use also showed no differences between pregnant women and all women ages 15 to 44. However, pregnant women were significantly less likely to use alcohol (any use or heavy use), cigarettes, and illicit drugs in the past month than other women of childbearing age. Among pregnant women, 1.8 percent used an illicit drug within the past month, compared with 6.7 percent of all women ages 15 to 44. Among all women with children, the rate is 5.2 percent. This finding supports efforts to intervene with pregnant substance abusers. A similar pattern is seen for use of alcohol and cigarettes. Fifty-four percent of women ages 15 to 44 were current drinkers, but 23 percent of pregnant women were drinkers in the past month. The rate of heavy alcohol use was 3.9 percent among women 15 to 44, but only 0.3 percent among pregnant women. The data indicate that pregnant women have more difficulty trying to reduce their cigarette use than their alcohol or illicit drug use. Twenty-one percent of pregnant women were current smokers compared with 31 percent of all women ages 15 to 44. Results were tested to make certain that age and marital status differences did not account for them (Women without children are generally younger and less likely to be married than pregnant women; women with children are generally older than pregnant women). The patterns persist after adjusting for differences in the age and marital status distribution of pregnant women, nonpregnant women with children, and nonpregnant women without children. This adjustment was made to the data for nonpregnant women, making their distribution similar to that of pregnant women. For example, after adjusting for age and marital status, 8.3 percent of nonpregnant women with no children were current illicit drug users in 1994, and 6.7 percent of nonpregnant women with children were current illicit drug users. Adjusted rates of lifetime use indicate that pregnant women, nonpregnant women with children, and nonpregnant women without children have similar patterns. Rates of illicit drug use were 46 percent, 47 percent, and 49 percent for these three groups, respectively.

As mentioned, the connection between domestic violence and substance use among women needs further study. A woman is beaten every 15 seconds.[2] Domestic violence is the leading cause of injury to women between the ages of 15 and 44 in the United States, more than car accidents, muggings, and rapes combined.[3] Battered women are more likely to suffer miscarriages and to give birth to babies with low birth weights.[4] Sixty-three percent of the young men between the ages of 11 and 20 who are serving time for homicide have killed their mother's abuser.[5] There are nearly three times as many animal shelters in the United States as there are shelters for battered women and their children.[6] Nationally, 50 percent of all homeless women and children are on the streets because of violence in the home.[7]

Recent research findings indicate that brutality and cruelty to children can leave a mark on the chemistry of the brain, which scientists conjecture may be what starts children on the road to becoming violent adults.

One animal study that was particularly telling showed that normally mild-mannered golden hamsters that were threatened and attacked when they were young, and that grew up to be cowardly bullies, had lasting changes in the brain circuitry for two neurotransmitters that regulate aggression. . . . And parallel data from several long-range studies of large groups of children show that those who were childhood victims of abuse or neglect were the most violent as teenagers.[8]

It is generally acknowledged that abused children become abusing adults. Prevailing studies implicate changes in serotonin or related neurotransmitter systems that demonstrate children who were abused or otherwise severely stressed in childhood were far more likely than others to be violent as teenagers or adults. Psychologist Cathy Spatz Widom of the State University of New York identified 908 childhood victims of criminal neglect or physical abuse where there was a record of criminal charges filed against the abuser. She tracked the children's criminal records over a 20-year period and concluded that those who were childhood victims of neglect had 50 percent more arrests for violent crimes than a comparison group, while for those who suffered physical abuse, the rate of violent crimes was double that of the comparison group.[9]

Another study by Adrian Raine, a psychologist at the University of Southern California, reported that 4,269 boys who suffered some form of birth complication and whose mothers were abusive or neglectful in infancy were three times as likely to be arrested for a violent crime by the age of 18. Raine noted that shaking a child vigorously is particularly damaging: "We know that can lead to laceration of the white nerve fibers that link the prefrontal cortex to deeper brain structures like the amygdala, which are involved in the generation of aggressive impulses, while the prefrontal lobes inhibit those impulses."[10]

The prevalence of domestic violence has caught the public's attention, but there are only 25 states that require arrest when a reported domestic dispute turns violent, and these laws are often underenforced, with police often leaving the site of violence when a victim does not want to press charges. Women are at greater risk of being killed by their current or former male partners than of any other kind of assault. Figure 10.8 lists prevalence by percentage of aggressive acts for men and women, and Figures 10.9 through 10.11 list types, ages, and race and ethnicity of substantiated maltreatment. Of 5,745 women murdered in 1991, six out of ten were killed by someone they knew, with half murdered by a spouse or someone with whom they had been intimate.[11]

While a small percentage of assaults on women result in death, the violence often involves severe physical or psychological damage. See Figure 10.12 for statistics of murder in families.

Women are in the most danger when they seek to put a firm end to an abusive relationship. See Figure 10.8 for prevalence of aggressive acts by men and women. Experts warn that the two actions most likely to trigger deadly assault are moving out of a shared residence and beginning a relationship with another man. There may be other psycho-physiological links to violence–alcohol and drug abuse often go hand-in-hand with spousal abuse, as does mental illness.

FIGURE 10.8. Prevalence by Percentage of Aggressive Acts for Men and Women

	Premarriage		18 Months		20 Months	
Variable	Men	Women	Men	Women	Men	Women
Throwing something at partner	6.8	12.6	8.1	14.2	7.3	14.2
Pushing, grabbing, or shoving	27.5	32.2	18.9	28.1	21.4	22.9
Slapping	7.7	20.7	6.2	15.8	5.7	10.7
Kicking, biting, or hitting with fist	3.4	12.6	3.9	10.8	2.7	7.6
Beating up	0.0	1.1	0.8	0.8	0.4	1.1
Threatening with knife or gun	0.0	0.0	0.0	0.7	0.4	1.5
Overall	31.2	44.4	26.8	35.9	24.6	32.2

Source: Journal of Family Violence, 41(2), 1989.

FIGURE 10.9. Types of Substantiated Maltreatment

	1990		1991	
	Number	Percent	Number	Percent
Type of maltreatment				
Neglect	358,846	44.8	366,462	44.7
Physical abuse	205,057	25.6	206,235	25.2
Sexual abuse	127,853	16.0	129,425	15.8
Emotional maltreatment	47,673	6.0	46,334	5.7
Other and unknown	61,714	7.7	71,466	8.7
Victims, total[†]	801,143	(X)	819,922	(X)
Gender of victim				
Male	360,531	46.5	376,617	46.1
Female	409,286	52.8	434,729	53.3
Unknown	4,779	0.7	4,877	0.6
Victims, total	775,596	100.0	816,223	100.0

[†]More than one type of maltreatment may be substantiated per child; therefore, the total for this item adds up to more than 100.

Source: U.S. Department of Health and Human Services, National Center on Child Abuse and Neglect, National Child Abuse and Neglect Data System, "Working Paper 2, 1991, Summary Data Component," May 1993; "Working Paper 2, 1992 Summary Data Component," May 1994.

Men have, in general, been socialized to hide their innermost thoughts and feelings. As young boys they were socialized to believe that if they were open about their feelings, they would be considered weak and unmanly. See Figure 10.13 for a profile of a male batterer.

Battering is not a momentary loss of temper, but rather the assertion of control in a relationship through fear, violence, and other forms of abuse. A batterer uses acts of violence and a series of behaviors, including intimidation, threats, psychological abuse, and isolation, to coerce and control the other person. The violence may not happen often, but it remains as a hidden and constant terror. One

FIGURE 10.10. Ages of Substantiated Maltreatment Victims

Age of Victim				
1 year and younger	107,217	13.6	112,227	13.8
2 to 5 years old	194,485	24.7	208,183	25.6
6 to 9 years old	177,396	22.5	189,124	23.3
10 to 13 years old	151,971	19.3	162,049	19.9
14 to 17 years old	117,312	14.9	122,603	15.1
18 and over	7,184	0.9	6,327	0.8
Unknown	32,773	4.2	12,544	1.5
Victims, total[†]	788,338	100.0	813,057	100.0

[†]More than one type of maltreatment may be substantiated per child; therefore, the total for this item adds up to more than 100.

Source: U.S. Department of Health and Human Services, National Center on Child Abuse and Neglect, National Child Abuse and Neglect Data System, "Working Paper 2, 1991, Summary Data Component," May 1993; "Working Paper 2, 1992 Summery Data Component," May 1994.

FIGURE 10.11. Race/Ethnicity of Substantiated Maltreatment Victims

White	424,470	54.7	454,059	55.5
Black	197,400	25.5	218,044	26.6
Asian and Pacific Islander	6,408	0.8	6,585	0.8
American Indian, Eskimo	10,283	1.3	10,873	1.3
Other races	11,749	1.5	12,982	1.6
Hispanic origin	73,132	9.4	77,985	9.5
Unknown	51,967	6.7	37,999	4.6
Victims, total	775,409	100.0	818,527	99.9

Source: U.S. Department of Health and Human Services, National Center on Child Abuse and Neglect, National Child Abuse and Neglect Data System, "Working Paper 2, 1991, Summary Data Component," May 1993; "Working Paper 2, 1992 Summary Data Component," May 1994.

FIGURE 10.12. Murder in Families

	Males	Females
Murder victims in domestic violence	55.5	44.5
Spouses acquitted for murder of a spouse	1.4	12.9
Spouses who receive probation for murdering a spouse	1.6	16.0
Average sentence (in years) for murdering a spouse	17.0	6.0
When children are murdered, 61 percent of the time it is by the mother.		

Source: U.S. Department of Justice, July 1994.

FIGURE 10.13. Profile of a Male Batterer from Clinical Practice

- Has low self-esteem
- Believes all the myths about battering relationships
- Is a traditionalist in male supremacy and the stereotyped masculine sex role in the family
- Blames others for his actions
- Is pathologically jealous
- Presents a dual personality
- Experiences severe stress reactions, during which he uses drinking and wife battering to cope
- Frequently uses sex as an act of aggression to enhance self-esteem in view of waning virility
- Does not believe his violent behavior should have negative consequences

in five women victimized by their spouses or ex-spouses report that they had been victimized over and over again by the same person.[12] Approximately one-third of the men counseled for battering at one treatment facility are professionals such as doctors, psychologists, lawyers, ministers, and business executives.[13] One in four pregnant women have a history of partner violence. Women who leave their batterers are at a 75 percent greater risk of being killed by the batterer than those who stay. Over two-thirds of violent victimizations against women are committed by someone known to them. See Figures 10.14 and 10.15 for data on rape victim's relationship to rapist and ages of victims. The U.S. Department of Justice reported that six times as many women victimized by intimates as those victimized by strangers did not report their violent victimization to police because they feared reprisal from the offender.

Battered women seek medical attention for injuries sustained as a consequence of domestic violence significantly more often after

FIGURE 10.14. Rape Victim's Relationship to Rapist

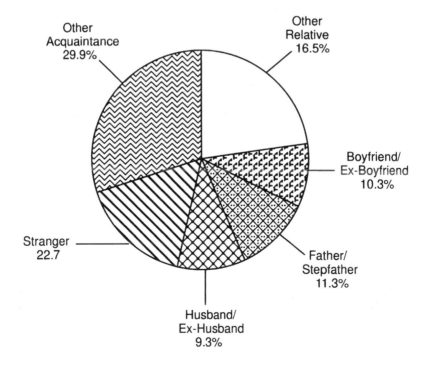

Other Acquaintance 29.9%

Other Relative 16.5%

Boyfriend/ Ex-Boyfriend 10.3%

Stranger 22.7

Father/ Stepfather 11.3%

Husband/ Ex-Husband 9.3%

Source: Time, May 4, 1992.

FIGURE 10.15. Rape Victim's Age

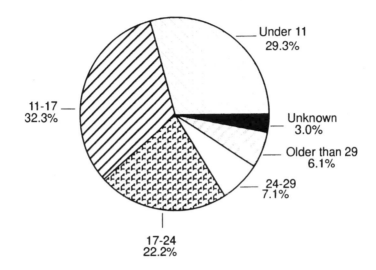

Under 11
29.3%

11-17
32.3%

Unknown
3.0%

Older than 29
6.1%

24-29
7.1%

17-24
22.2%

Source: Time, May 4, 1992.

separation than during cohabitation. Approximately 75 percent of emergency room visits by battered women occur after separation, and three-quarters of calls to law enforcement for intervention and assistance in domestic violence occur after separation from batterers. One study revealed that half of the homicides of female spouses and partners were committed by men after separation from batterers.[14] Businesses forfeit another $100 million in lost wages, sick leave, absenteeism, and non-productivity.[15] It is estimated that 25 percent of workplace problems such as absenteeism, lower productivity, turnover, and excessive use of medical benefits are due to family violence. Violence is the reason stated for divorce in 22% of middle-class marriages.[16]

The National Institute of Allergy and Infectious Diseases (NIAID) reported at the end of 1994 that HIV-infected women are one-third more likely to die without an AIDS-defining condition than are HIV-infected men. Investigators could not identify why the women had a greater risk of relatively early death, but conjecture that important factors may include poorer access to or use of health care resources among HIV-infected women as compared to men, domestic violence, and lack of social supports for women. The findings stem from 15 months of observations of more than 4,500 people enrolled in a prospective study of HIV disease progression and survival. HIV disease among women in the United States represents nearly 13 percent of all cases, a more than 20-fold increase since 1981. HIV disease is the leading cause of death in New York City for women ages 25 to 44, and among the top five leading causes of death for other U.S. women of the same age. The inequality of women in our culture affects every aspect of the HIV pandemic and, in part, has resulted in the current orphanization of children.

NOTES

1. K. Tardiff, P.M. Marzuk, A.C. Leon, C.S. Hirsch, M. Stajic, L. Portera, and N. Hartwell, Homicide in New York City: Cocaine Use and Firearms. *Journal of the American Medical Association* 1994;272:43-46.

2. U.S. Department of Justice, Bureau of Justice Statistics, Washington, DC, October 1983.

3. Uniform Crime Reports, Federal Bureau of Investigation, 1991.

4. Surgeon General, United States, 1992.

5. March of Dimes, 1992.

6. Senate Judiciary Hearings, Violence Against Women Act, 1990.

7. U.S. Senate Committee on the Judiciary, Violence Against Women: Victims of the System, 1991.

8. D. Goleman, "Early Violence Leaves Its Mark on the Brain," *The New York Times* October 3, 1995.

9. *Op Cit.*

10. *Op Cit.*

11. J. Smolowe, "When Violence Hits Home," *Time* July 1, 1994.

12. Uniform Crime Reports, Federal Bureau of Investigation (FBI), 1990.

13. Surgeon General Antonia Novello, as quoted in *Domestic Violence: Battered Women*, publication of the Reference Department of the Cambridge Public Library, Cambridge, MA.

14. B. Hart, Remarks to the Task Force on Child Abuse and Neglect, April 1992.

15. *Domestic Violence for Health Care Providers,* 3rd Edition, Colorado Domestic Violence Coalition, 1991.

16. *Employee Assistance Program Digest* November/December 1991.

Chapter 11

At Certain Hours
It Haunts the House

My children cause me the most exquisite suffering of which I have any experience. It is the suffering of ambivalence: the murderous alternation between bitter resentment and raw-edged nerves, and blissful gratification and tenderness. Sometimes I seem to myself, in my feelings toward these tiny guiltless beings, a monster of selfishness and intolerance.

Adrienne Rich, *Of Woman Born*

In 1989, an agency whose basic mission was to provide reproductive health organized a support group for HIV-positive women in downtown Brooklyn at a time when there were few services for women affected by the epidemic. Michelle was a founding member of this group, and now, almost six years later, she remains healthy, living with HIV disease, raising two teenage children. Her husband, Joe, is also HIV positive.

They decided to engage in couple therapy almost a year ago because their marriage of nearly 20 years was deteriorating under the burden of their mutual diagnosis. Neither of their children know of their HIV serostatus. The problems of the relationship were always present but went unaddressed, with years of mutual intravenous substance use masking the symptoms of a failed marriage. They were bonded by a mutual partnership of getting and using heroin, discovering that they were virtual strangers after joining Narcotics Anonymous (NA). Without drugs, Joe resorted to the addiction of compulsive gambling with the identical fervor, destructiveness, and secrecy. Michelle became addicted to credit card spending.

The family balanced financial ruin by balancing credit cards to pay credit cards. For Joe, gambling provided the excitement of the chase and the intoxicating escape from reality. For Michelle, credit cards created the illusion of affluence and class. She traveled from Brooklyn to Manhattan for shopping sprees in expensive department stores, ending the excursion in exclusive hair salons. She gave the children anything they wanted to assuage her guilt for neglecting them during their formative years while she was actively using drugs. Joe, burdened with guilt for a failed life, sank into gambling dens, disappearing for unaccounted hours.

Both were valiant in their attempts to understand and change their destructive behavior, but HIV disease hung like a cloud over their lives, so the addictions were sometimes viewed as their reward. They spoke of separation, but the bond between them was not completely severed—there was an unspoken commitment to be together to the end. The couple therapy ended abruptly when Joe began experiencing merciless, debilitating headaches and periods of disorientation. One afternoon, Michelle was called at her job by a hospital emergency department when Joe was driving the wrong way on a Brooklyn street and crashed his car into a storefront. He was taken to be evaluated, and discharged with minor cuts that required some stitching. He had an anxiety attack, weeping uncontrollably and incoherently, and required an injection of valium.

Within the week, at Michelle's insistence, Joe went to his infectious disease physician. He was terrified to get a diagnosis, suspecting the worst. And the worst followed a CAT scan in which demyelination was found in the white matter of his brain. Joe was diagnosed with progressive multifocal leukoencephalopathy (PML), which is an HIV disease-related opportunistic infection (OI), a type of AIDS dementia complex, and a viral infection of the brain that causes memory loss, motor control problems, and loss of strength. PML can lead to a coma from which there is progressive decline until death.

He was diagnosed during a hospitalization, and when the doctor told him, he thought of the infamous Mafia code of *omerta*, or silence, not wanting to tell Michelle of what lay before them. But the decline was so rapid that he quickly became unable to have control over any decision making. Michelle thought what a wonderful fact to reflect on, that every human is constituted to be that profound secret and mystery to every other. A solemn consideration, when she entered the hospital room late one night, that every one of us has his or her secret. In Narcotics Anonymous, she re-called, there is an expression, "You are as sick as your secrets." The door to Joe's room was half-opened, secured at an angle, allowing a broad ray of light from the hallway into the dark room and revealing Joe as an apparition. His beard had become gray, raggedly cut, but not very long, his face was hollow, and his eyes were exceedingly bright. His hospital gown lay open at the throat, and showed his body to be withered and worn. In seclusion from direct light and air, he appeared faded to a dull uniformity of parchment yellow. He had put up a hand between his eyes and the light, and the very bones of it seemed transparent. So he sat, with a steadfastly vacant gaze. He never looked at Michelle, standing before him, without first looking down on one side of himself, then on the other, as if he had lost the habit of associating place with sound. No human intelligence could have read the mysteries of his mind in the scared blank wonder of his face. Whether he knew what had happened, whether he recollected what they had said to him, whether he knew that he was free, were questions which no one could have answered.

Joe Jr. and Lana tried speaking to him, but he was so confused, and so very slow to answer, that they became frightened at his bewilderment, and agreed for the time to tamper with him no more. He had a wild, lost manner of occasionally clasping his head in his hands, that had not been seen in him before; yet, he had some pleasure in the mere sound of his daughter's voice, and invariably turned to it when she spoke. He was now a captive of many years of silence, with only the faintest sign of an actively intent intelligence remaining in his eyes. Michelle had crept along the wall to a point where she could see him, and where she now stood looking at him, first with hands raised in frightened compassion, then extended toward him, trembling with eagerness to lay the spectral face upon her warm young breast, and love it back to life and hope. So exactly was Joe's expression repeated (though with greater strength) on her fair young face, that it looked as though it had passed like a moving light, from him to her.

Michelle asked me to come to her home to sit with her and the children while she told them of Joe's prognosis and that, she too, was HIV positive. Bensonhurst is a section of Brooklyn that is mostly Italian, the scene of racial discord several years ago with the murder of Yusuf Hawkins. The 16-year-old Brooklyn boy's death was a national reminder of streets in white America where an African American dares not tread. It was Hawkins' misfortune to have set foot on such a street in the Bensonhurst section of Brooklyn that fateful night. He and some friends had entered the largely Italian, working-class neighborhood to inspect a used car advertised for sale there. They were suddenly surrounded by ten or so white youths. Inflamed by the fact that a former girlfriend of their ringleader was associating with blacks and Hispanics, the whites were looking for trouble. They carried baseball bats and at least one gun. It was fired four times. Hawkins died shortly afterward. When scores of blacks marched into Bensonhurst to protest the slaying, numerous residents screamed at the protesters, "Niggers, go home!" and mockingly held aloft watermelons.

At the time of early European exploration this site of Brooklyn was occupied by the Canarsie people, an Algonquian-speaking group. Bensonhurst is a community not dissimilar from many other New York City neighborhoods that have undergone a dramatic ethnic or racial transformation. If you look south on any main avenue, the top spires of the Verrazano-Narrows Bridge can be seen beyond the foreground buildings. The bridge is the longest vehicular suspension in the United States, spanning the Narrows from Brooklyn to Staten Island at the entrance to New York harbor. Completed in 1964, the bridge, providing easy access to the underdeveloped Staten Island, generated a wave of blue-collar urban flight from the city to predominantly Caucasian communities. For most of this century, Italian-Americans lived in Sunset Park, wedged between Bay Ridge and Park Slope, a few blocks from the East River, and crisscrossed by parkways that traverse the borough. Adjacent to the Belt Parkway and close to the piers by the river is an underpass well-known for illicit drug-procuring and female prostitution. The train ride gave me the opportunity to think of the long-running adversarial relationship between blacks and Italians in this area.

Michelle and Joe met when they were high school seniors—they were insignificantly related, cousins many times removed. The attraction was immediate and intemperately sexual, and they couldn't satiate their desire for one another. Joe had experimented with heroin use several months before meeting Michelle, and he introduced the narcotic into the relationship one night after they had been to a movie and walked along the promenade at Brooklyn Heights. There was no need for deception because there was little Michelle wouldn't do for Joe, who represented an escape from her family. Within months, heroin replaced eroticism and finding the money and dealer became the focus or their relationship. They'd park the car, inject drugs, and nod out until dawn.

A week before Thanksgiving, Joe robbed his family, taking gifts that his mother, Estelle, had wrapped for Christmas and had hidden on a closet shelf, along with a 20-pound turkey from a freezer chest in the basement. Despite her initial denial, his mother was eventually no longer willing to tolerate Joe's behavior, and she threatened to ban him from her home. Joe made plans to visit an uncle in Florida, where he intended to detoxify from drugs, and he asked Michelle to accompany him. There was one condition: she demanded that they go as a married couple, so six months into the relationship, they married. Joe's mother was ecstatic, believing marriage would stabilize her son. The marriage took place in Estelle's home, and Joe and Michelle took their vows anesthetized by drugs. The blurred memory of the wedding that joined them in weakness deteriorated during the months in Florida. They experienced withdrawal during the first weeks, incriminating each other into blame for years of addiction through an onslaught of verbal taunts. By the second month, they were using drugs again, and, when high, the relationship returned to normalcy. They returned to New York after exhausting the uncle's hospitality, and Michelle learned she was pregnant.

A few months after they returned to New York, Joe, almost unemployable, was hired to be a security guard by a private security company. He received minimal training and most of the other guards were active or intermittent substance users. They moved to Alphabet City, the euphemistic name for the Lower East Side of Manhattan, living in a tenement apartment on Avenue B. The building was without central heating; instead, there were gas-generated space heaters in two of the four railroad flat rooms. They were desperate for living quarters, and it was the middle of a searingly hot summer, generating the type of white heat that seems to liquefy tar pavement.

Joe's first security guard assignment was at the entrance to a privately owned methadone maintenance clinic, informally known as Dr. D's. Dr. D was a physician in his early seventies, and past his prime to practice medicine. Dispensing methadone was profitable in the 1960s, and while the state regulated the legally controlled substance, there were no treatment or medical services for patients. Patients could self-pay or use Medicaid, and they lined up around the block, particularly after a weekend, waiting for the clinic to open. Joe began to purchase methadone from patients when he or Michelle couldn't procure heroin. The methadone wasn't pure; Joe could tell that it was diluted when withdrawal symptoms were acutely uncomfortable, and the methadone didn't help. Patients would swallow some of the methadone, spitting the remainder into the small bottle, trying to reseal the cap.

Lana was born during an Indian summer. When Michelle and Joe returned from the hospital, they put Lana to bed in one of the single beds in their bedroom and left the door half-open, falling asleep in the living room as a broad ray of light fell into the room. Michelle was startled awake by the vision of a man with a white beard, raggedly cut, but not very long, a hollow face, and exceedingly bright eyes. She knew intuitively that it was a visitation of death, but shrugged it off as she had so many other visions before.

After many years of injection drug use, Michelle prided herself on being able to get Joe off: "I used to inject him. I was an expert at it. Yeah, even friends would have me do it for them. And the dealer, too. He'd get us the dope, and I would get him off." She studied the track marks, long obliterated scars of an actively intent intelligence, some fainter, hoping to see them all gone, but they were there as an immutable reminder. She remembered raising Lana from the bassinet with frightened compassion, trembling with eagerness, wanting to love her back to life and hope, but within a week Joe and Michelle relapsed into drug use, completely out of control, worse than before. No human intelligence could have read the mysteries of her mind, in the scared blank wonder of her face, as she recollected the early years of her first child's life. She had a wild, lost manner of occasionally clasping her head in her hands, remembering the years of drug use, speaking of it as if it were the submissive behavior of one long accustomed to obeying under coercion.

"I don't know how we survived. Joe worked though, never missing a day as a security guard, so we always had a roof and food on the table. But drugs were all that mattered. Joe and me fought all the time, always accusing each other for our addiction, never trusting one another." She physically held back emotions, putting her hands into her pants pockets, as she meditated on a misspent life. "I don't know how Lana survived. I guess children are strong, but I used to ignore her, and when she cried it would make me crazy. By the time Joey was born, we had nothing left, no money, no self-respect. I don't remember conceiving him—we had sex so infrequently. It took eight more years for us to get clean. Joey was about eight. I went to school on parent's day, high out of my mind, and I saw the look of horror on his face. Within the week, I went to Narcotics Anonymous and Joe followed me within days. I've been clean for seven years. Except for a one-day relapse, it's been continuous. I took a job as a medical technician. Well, the temptation was too much, with all the drugs right there. I injected myself with valium and nearly passed out in the doctor's office.

"We thought about a third child—to make up for the past, a child in sobriety. We really couldn't afford to have a third." Michelle did not want to look ahead, the prospect of her life made her feel as if she were buried alive. She said very little to her husband, but her manner toward him had changed. He began chemotherapy, treatments every four weeks: he lost his hair, shaved the beard, had to have a catheter inserted. He felt emasculated. She had never despised her husband, but turned her attention to the children. As she turned from him, he began to neglect her; his home as he knew it was gone. What he felt just at the minute, that was all to him. He could not abide anything. There was nothing behind all his show. There began a battle between the husband and wife—a fearful, bloody battle that ended only with the death of one. She fought to make him undertake his own responsibilities, to make him fulfill his obligations. But he was too different from her. His nature was purely sensuous, and she strove to make him moral, religious. She tried to force him to face things. He could not endure it—it drove him out of his mind. Something in her proud, honorable soul had crystallized hard as rock.

His masculine clumsiness pierced her heart while she fought against him bitterly; she worried about him, as if he had gone astray from her. Now she ceased to want his love: he became an outsider to her. This made life much more bearable. Nevertheless, she still continued to strive with him. She still had her high moral sense, now a religious instinct, and she was almost a fanatic with him, because she loved him, or had loved him. If he sinned, she tortured him. If he gambled and lied, she tongue-lashed him unmercifully. The pity was, she was too much his opposite. She could not be content with the little he might be; she would have him be the man that he ought to be. So, in seeking to make him nobler than he could be, she destroyed him. She injured and hurt and scarred herself, but she lost none of her worth. She also had the children.

The train swerved abruptly as it left the underground tunnel for the elevated outdoors. It was the week of the Blizzard of '96 when two feet of snow hit New York City, the largest snowstorm in the last 50 years, and this section of Brooklyn–Bensonhurst–was completely snowed under. The sun glaringly refracted light on the mounds of snow on rooftops into the subway car. Michelle and Joe lived about a block from the train station, and during the brief walk I was able to get a sense of the neighborhood, which seemed forsaken in a time warp somewhere in the 1960s. Their apartment seemed familiar from the many descriptions Michelle brought to session—the time she stripped to the natural finish a door separating the living room and their bedroom, the tiles she laid in the kitchen, and their dog Barney, a friendly boxer who barked a greeting as I entered the front door.

I had met Joe Jr. before, when he insisted on coming to a session unannounced to show his parents a deplorable report card the week before he was to leave on a trip to the Bahamas. This would be my first meeting with Lana. Michelle had called me in a panic when Joe was hospitalized again the previous week. She said: "I have to tell the children. I can't keep the secret any longer. Will you come to Brooklyn to meet with them? They won't come to your office."

Children usually do not talk about their feelings: instead, they show feelings through behavior. Michelle had received a call from Joe Jr.'s high school teacher saying she was at wit's end, declaring that he was the "ringleader who's disrupting the class." School problems are a certain indicator that a child is upset. Another sign is fighting. Michelle said, "Lana doesn't leave the house; all she does is sleep and eat." Some children are noisy and aggressive; others refuse to go outside the home and are quiet and withdrawn.

We sat in the living room, the four of us. Joe Jr. wore a Tommy Hilfiger hat with his head bowed—his leg pumped vigorously as if he had no control over its motion. Lana stared into space with no apparent affect. Michelle's face seemed to contain anger, alarm, bewilderment, and a hint of consternation. She had to reach past any sense of being defective or defeated to tell her children that their father has HIV disease.

Michelle began: "I've wanted to protect you both from the truth for a while. But I think you both need to know something. I didn't want to hurt you or cause you any pain." She was interrupted by Lana's weeping and Joe Jr.'s beginning to cry; she, too, began to cry, but found the strength to continue. "Your father has AIDS. I care for you both and wanted to protect you. Everything is being done for him, but it doesn't look good. I love you both." The weight of years left her as she understood that it was normal for them to have strong feelings.

Lana said, "I've known for a couple of years. All your friends go to the same doctor." Joe Jr. joined with, "I guess I knew but I put it out of my head." After the three cried for a while, they asked very typical questions about how long he had been infected and what could be done medically.

The family was emotionally shattered and the years of dysfunctionality seemed unimportant as they wept and held each other. They needed to be alone. I left their Brooklyn home feeling bewildered by the enormity of pain and suffering I had witnessed. Michelle was incapable of telling the children about her own HIV status; that would be for another time, another time soon. I would be there.

Adoption Resources

ADOPTION ORGANIZATIONS

ADOPTIVE FAMILIES OF AMERICA
3333 Highway 100 North
Minneapolis, MN 55422
612-535-4829

AFA's mission is to provide problem-solving assistance and information about the challenges of adoption to members of adoptive and prospective adoptive families. AFA seeks to create opportunities for successful adoptive placement and promotes the health and welfare of children without permanent families.

ALMA (Adoptees Liberty Movement Association)
P.O. Box 727 Radio City Station
New York, NY 10101-0727
212-581-1568
Search and reunion support and national registry

AMERICAN ADOPTION CONGRESS
1000 Connecticut Avenue, NW, Suite 9
Washington, DC 20036
202-483-3399
Search and reunion information and referrals

CONCERNED UNITED BIRTH PARENTS
2000 Walker Street
Des Moines, IA 50317
800-822-2777
Birth parents support group

INTERNATIONAL SOUNDEX REUNION REGISTRY–ISRR
P.O. Box 2312
Carson City, NV 89702
702-882-7755
Mutual consent registry

KINSHIP ALLIANCE
513 E. First Street
Tustin, CA 92680
714-573-8865
Professional association that provides adoption training

LATIN AMERICAN ADOPTIVE FAMILIES
23 Evangeline Road
Falmouth, MA 02540
508-548-1963
Support and resources for adoptive parents of children from Latin
America

LATIN AMERICAN PARENTS ASSOCIATION
P.O. Box 523
Unionville, CT 06085
203-270-1424
Adoptive parent support group

LATIN AMERICAN PARENTS ASSOCIATION, NATIONAL
CAPITAL REGION
P.O. Box 4403
Silver Spring, MD 20914
301-431-3407
Adoptive parent support group

NATIONAL FEDERATION FOR OPEN ADOPTION EDUCATION
391 Taylor Boulevard, Suite 100
Pleasant Hill, CA 94523
510-827-2229
Promotes open adoptions through training and advocacy

NATIONAL FOSTER PARENT ASSOCIATION
226 Kilts Drive
Houston, TX 77024-6214
713-467-1850
Provides information and support for foster parents

NORTH AMERICAN COUNCIL ON ADOPTABLE CHILDREN
970 Raymond Avenue, Suite 106
St. Paul, MN 55114-1149
612-644-3036
Professional organization concerned with adoption—sponsors yearly conference

SINGLE ADOPTIVE PARENTS
P.O. Box 15084
Chevy Chase, MD 20825
Support and advice for those adopting alone

ADOPTION PRINT RESOURCES

ADOPTALK
NACAC
1821 University Avenue, Suite 498
St. Paul, MN 55104
Quarterly—information about special needs adoption, foster care, and federal legislation

ADOPTED CHILD
Lois Melina
P.O. Box 9362
Moscow, ID 83843
208-882-1794
4-page newsletter for adoptive parents discussing one topic, in-depth, per month

ADOPTION FACTBOOK
National Council for Adoption
1930 17th Street NW
Washington, DC 20009
202-328-1200
Annual–U.S. statistics on adoption

ADOPTION HELPER
189 Springdale Boulevard
Toronto, Ontario M4C 1Z6
Canada
Bimonthly magazine for Canadian adoptive parents

ADOPTION MEDICAL NEWS
Adoptions Advocates Press
1921 Ohio Street NE
Palm Bay, FL 32907
407-725-6379
Medical information for families, adoption experts, and doctors

ADOPTION REPORT
Child Welfare League of America
440 First Street, NW
Washington, DC 20001

ADOPTION THERAPIST
800-944-4460
Concentrating on the psychological aspects of adoption

ADOPTION TRIAD FORUM
Alicia Lanier
P.O. Box 832161
Richardson, TX 75083
214-699-1269

ADOPTION UPDATE
National Adoption Center
1218 Chestnut Street
Philadelphia, PA 19107
800-TO-ADOPT
Free biannual newsletter about minority and special needs adoption

ADOPTIVE FAMILIES
Adoptive Families of America
3333 Highway 100 N
Minneapolis, MN 55422
800-373-3300
Bimonthly magazine for adoptive parents

ALMA SEARCHLIGHT
ALMA
P.O. Box 727, Radio City Station
New York, NY 10101
212-581-1568
Adoptee's Liberty Movement Association newsletter

CHAIN OF LIFE
Janine Baer
P.O. Box 8081
Berkeley, CA 94707
Bimonthly magazine with feminist/gay/lesbian focus

DECREE
American Adoption Congress
1000 Connecticut Avenue, NW, Suite 9
Washington, DC 20036

FRIENDS OF THE COURT
800-717-5717
Newsletter of the Adoption Studies Institute

JEWEL AMONG JEWELS
9302 Seascape Drive
Indianapolis, IN 46256
Christian-oriented newsletter for adoptees

LATIN AMERICAN ADOPTIVE FAMILIES
23 Evangeline Road
Falmouth, MA 02540
Quarterly magazine about adoption from Latin America

LIFELINES
Bethany Christian Services
901 Eastern Avenue NE
Grand Rapids, MI 49503
Published by Bethany Christian Services

NATIONAL ADOPTION AWARENESS CONVENTION
P.O. Box 2823
Chapel Hill, NC
919-967-5010
Quarterly newsletter

NATIONAL ADOPTION REPORTS
National Council for Adoption
1930 17th Street NW
Washington, DC 20009
202-328-1200
Quarterly newsletter of the National Council for Adoption

ON THE VINE
Rebecca Dalton
P.O. Box 1852
Appleton, WI 54913
For birthmothers of children who are still minors

OPEN ADOPTION BIRTHPARENT
Brenda Romanchik
R-Squared Press
721 Hawthorne Street
Royal Oak, MI 48067
For birthparents involved in open adoptions

PEOPLE SEARCHING NEWS
P.O. Box 100444
Palm Bay, FL 32910
Bimonthly magazine focusing on search issues

QUEST
Kinquest
P.O. Box 873
Bowling Green Station
New York, NY 10274

REPORT ON FOREIGN ADOPTION
Anna Marie Merril
ICCC
911 Cypress Drive
Boulder, CO 80303
303-494-8439
Bimonthly updates on adopting internationally

REUNIONS: THE MAGAZINE
Edith Wagner
P.O. Box 11727
Milwaukee, WI 53211
Bimonthly magazine on search and reunion

ROOTS AND WINGS
Cynthia Peck
P.O. Box 638
Chester, NJ 07930
Quarterly magazine of interest to all members of
The Adoption Triad

SEARCHING RESOURCE
Carol Robertson
15420 Olde Highway 80
Space #151
El Cajon, CA 92021
For those beginning a search

Bibliography

Allport, G. W. (1987). *The Nature of Prejudice.* Reading, MA: Addison-Wesley.

Amaro, H. and Gornemann, I. (1992). HIV/AIDS-related Knowledge, Attitudes, Beliefs and Behaviors Among Hispanics in the Northeast and Puerto Rico: Report of Findings and Recommendations. A Study Conducted by the Northeast Hispanic AIDS Consortium. Boston University School of Public Health.

Andrews, J.A., Hops, H., Ary, D., Tildesley, E., and Harris, J. (1993). Parental Influence on Early Adolescent Substance Use: Specific and Nonspecific Effects. *Journal of Early Adolescence* 13:285-310.

Aruffo, J.F., Coverdale, J.H., and Vallbona, C. (1991). AIDS Knowledge in Low-Income and Minority Populations. *Public Health Reports* 106(2):115-119.

Aust, P.H. (September-October, 1987). Using the Life Story Book in Treatment of Children in Placement. *Child Welfare* Vol. LX, no. 8, 535-560.

Bakeman, R., Lumb, J.R., Jackson, R.E., and Smith, D.W. (1987). AIDS Risk-group Profiles in Whites and Members of Minority Groups. *Journal of the American Medical Association* 257:191-192.

Bataille, G. (1962). *Death and Sensuality.* New York: Walker and Company.

Bayer, R. (1981). *Homosexuality and American Psychiatry.* New York: Basic Books.

Bayer, R. (1991). *Private Acts, Social Consequences: AIDS and the Politics of Public Health.* New Brunswick, NJ: Rutgers University Press.

Bayer, R. (1991). Public Health Policy and the AIDS Epidemic: An End to AIDS Exceptionalism? *New England Journal of Medicine* 324:1500-1504.

Beck, E. (1973). *The Denial of Death.* New York: The Free Press.

Benjamin, J. (1988). *The Bonds of Love.* New York: Pantheon Books.

Berreman, G.D. (1985). Race, Caste, and Other Invidious Distinctions in Social Stratification. In *Majority and Minority: The Dynamics of Race and Ethnicity* (N.R. Yetman, ed.) Boston: Allyn and Bacon, 21-39.

Biddlecom, A.E. and Hardy, A.M. (October 17, 1991). AIDS Knowledge and Attitudes of Hispanic Americans: United States, 1990. Provisional Data from the National Health Interview Survey. National Center for Health Statistics Advance Data.

Blackwell, J. (1985). *The Black Community: Diversity and Unity,* 2d ed. New York: Harper and Row.

Blanck, G. and R. (1974). *Ego Psychology: Theory and Practice.* New York: Columbia University Press.

Bowlby, J. (1980). *Attachment and Loss, Volumes I, II, and III.* New York: Basic Books.

Braithwaite, R. and Lythcott, N. (1989). Community Empowerment as a Strategy for Health Promotion for Black and Other Populations. *Journal of the American Medical Association* 261:282-283.

Brill, A.A. (1966). *The Basic Writings of Sigmund Freud.* New York: The Modern Library.

Brodzinsky, D.M. (1987). Adjustment to Adoption: A Psychosocial Perspective. In *Clinical Psychology Review* Vol. 7, 25-37.

Brodzinsky, D. and Schechter, M. (eds.) (1990). *The Psychology of Adoption.* New York: Oxford University Press.

Brook, J.S., Whiteman, M., Cohen, P., and Tanaka, J.S. (1991). Childhood Precursors of Adolescent Drug Use: A Longitudinal Analysis. *Genetic, Social, and General Psychology Monographs 11* 8(2): 195-213.

Brook, J.S., Whiteman, M., Gordon, A.S., and Brook, D.W. (1990). The Psychosocial Etiology of Adolescent Drug Use: A family Interactional Approach. *Genetic, Social, and General Psychology Monographs 11* 6(2):113-267.

Brook, J.S., Whiteman, M., Hamburg, B.A., and Balka, E.B. (1992). African-American and Puerto Rican Drug Use: Personality, Familial, and Other Environmental Risk Factors. *Genetic, Social, and General Psychology Monographs 11* 8(4):417-438.

Brown, Norman O. (1969). *Life Against Death.* Middleton, CT: Wesleyan University Press.

Brownmiller, S. (1975). *Against Our Will: Men, Women, and Rape.* New York: Simon and Schuster.

Burke, D.S., Brundage, J.F., Goldenbaum, M., Gardner, L.I., Peterson, M. , Visintine, R., Redfield, R.R. (1990). Human Immunodeficiency Virus Infections in Teenagers: Seroprevalence Among Applicants for U.S. Military Service. *Journal of the American Medical Association* 263:2074-2077.

Burkey, R.M. (1978). *Ethnic and Racial Groups: The Dynamics of Dominance.* Menlo Park, CA: Cummings.

Burns, D.N., Landesman, S., Muenz, L.R., Nugent, R.P., Goedert, J.J., Minkoff, H., Walsh, J.H., Mendez, H., Rubinstein, A., Willoughby, A. (1994). Cigarette Smoking, Premature Rupture of Membranes, and Vertical Transmission of HIV-1 Among Women with Low CD4+ Levels. *Journal of Acquired Immune Deficiency Syndrome* 7:718-726.

Caldwell, M.B., Fleming, P.L., and Oxtoby, M.J. (1992). Estimated Number of AIDS Orphans in the United States. *Pediatrics* 90(3): 482.

Carballo-Dieguez, A. (1989). Hispanic Culture, Gay Male Culture, and AIDS: Counseling Implications. *Journal of Counseling and Development* 68:26-30.

Castro, K. and Narkinas, J. (July/August, 1989). Seroprevalence of HIV Infection in Seasonal and Migrant Farmworkers: Preliminary results. Migrant Health Clinical Supplement, National Migrant Referral Project.

Centers for Disease Control (CDC). (1991a). Drug Use and Sexual Behaviors Among Sex Partners of Injection-drug Users, United States, 1988-1990. *Morbidity and Mortality Weekly Report* 40(49):855-860.

Centers for Disease Control (CDC). (1991b). Mortality Attributable to HIV Infection/AIDS, United States, 1981-1990. *Morbidity and Mortality Weekly Report* 40(3):41-44.

Centers for Disease Control (CDC). (1992). Selected Behaviors that Increase Risk for HIV Infection Among High School Students, United States, 1990. *Morbidity and Mortality Weekly Report* 41(14):231-240.

Chesler, P. (1972). *Women & Madness.* New York: Avon.

Chodorow, N.J. (1978). *The Reproduction of Mothering: Psycho-analysis and the Sociology of Gender.* Berkeley: University of California Press.

Chodorow, N.J. (1989). *Feminism and Psychoanalytic Theory.* New Haven: Yale University Press.

Chu, S.Y., Peterman, T.A., Doll, L.S., Buehler, J.W., and Curran, J.W. (1992). AIDS in Bisexual Men in the United States: Epidemiology and Transmission to Women. *American Journal of Public Health* 82(2):220-224.

Cordell, A.S., Nathan, C., and Krymon, V. (March-April, 1985). Group Counseling for Children Adopted at Older Ages. *Child Welfare,* vol. LXIV, no. 2, 113-124.

Dalton, H.L. (1989). AIDS in Black Face. *Daedalus* 118(3):205-227.

Dansky, S.F. (1970). Hey Man. *RAT* Newspaper, August.

Dansky, S.F. (1994). *Now Dare Everything: Tales of HIV-Related Psychotherapy.* Binghamton, NY: The Haworth Press.

Dansky, S.F., Knoebel, J., Pitchford, K. (1971). The Effeminist Manifesto. *Double-F Magazine.*

David, R.J. and Collins, J.W. (1991). Bad Outcomes in Black Babies: Race or Racism? *Ethnicity and Disease* 1:236-244.

Davis, Iris. (1993). Preface in Gynecological Care Manual for HIV-Positive Women, Risa Denenberg, FNP, Essential Medical Systems.

De Carpio, A.B., Carpio-Cedraro, F.F., and Anderson, L. (1990). Hispanic Families Learning and Teaching About AIDS: A Participatory Approach at Community Level. *Hispanic Journal of Behavioral Sciences* 12:165-176.

de la Cancela, V. (1989). Minority AIDS Prevention: Moving Beyond Cultural Perspectives Toward Socio-political Empowerment. *AIDS Education and Prevention* 1(2):141-153.

Des Jarlais, D.C., Friedman, S.R., Novick, D.M., Sotheran, J.L., Thomas, P., Yancovitz, S.R., Mildvan, D., Weber, J., Kreek, M.J., and Maslansky, R. (1989). HIV-1 Infection Among Intravenous Drug Users in Manhattan, New York City, from 1977 through 1987. *Journal of the American Medical Association* 261:1008-1012.

Domestic Violence for Health Care Providers, 3rd Edition. (1991). Colorado Domestic Violence Coalition.

Dorman, M. and Klein D. (1985). *How to Stay Two When Baby Makes Three*. New York: Ballantine Books.

Dunn, D.T., Newell, M.L., Ades, A.E., Peckham, C.S. (1992). Risk of Human Immunodeficiency Virus Type 1 Transmission Through Breastfeeding. *Lancet* 340:585-588.

Dunn, D.T., Newell, M.L. Mayaux, M.J., Kind, C., Hutto, C., Goedert, J.J., Andiman, W. (1994). Mode of Delivery and Vertical Transmission of HIV-1: A Review of Prospective Studies. *Journal of Acquired Immune Deficiency Syndrome* 7:1064-1066.

Easterbrook, P.J., Keruly, J.C., Creagh-Kirk, T., Richman, D.D., Chaisson, R.E., Moore, R.D. (1991). Racial and Ethnic Differences in Outcome in Zidovudine-treated Patients with Advanced HIV Disease. *Journal of the American Medical Association* 266:2713-2718.

Elder-Tabrizy, K.A., Wolitski, R.J., Rhodes, F., and Baker, J.G. (1991). AIDS and Competing Health Concerns of Blacks, Hispanics and Whites. *Journal of Community Health* 16:11-12.

El-Sadr, W. and Capps, L. (1992). The Challenge of Minority Recruitment in Clinical Trials for AIDS. *Journal of the American Medical Association* 267(7):954-958.

Employee Assistance Program Digest. (November/December 1991).

Ensminger, M.E. (1990). Sexual Activity and Problem Behaviors Among Black, Urban Adolescents. *Child Development* 61:2032-2046.

Ensminger, M.E., Brown, C.H., and Kellam, S.G. (1982). Sex Differences in Antecedents of Substance Use Among Adolescents. *Journal of Social Issues* 38(2):25-42.

Erikson, Erik H. (1963). *Childhood and Society*. New York, W. W. Norton.

Erikson, Erik H. (1980). *Identity and the Life Cycle*. New York: W. W. Norton.

Fahlberg, V. (1990). "Attachment and Separation" from the series, *Putting the Pieces Together*. Southfield, MI: Spaulding for Children.

Firestone, Shulamith. (1971). *The Dialectic of Sex*. New York: Bantam.

Fox, D.M. (1990). Chronic Disease and Disadvantage: The New Politics of HIV Infection. *Journal of Health Politics, Policy and Law* 15:341-355.

Fraiberg, S.H. (1984). *Magic Years: Understanding and Handling the Problems of Early Childhood.* New York: Charles Scribner's Sons.

Freudenberg, N., Lee, J., and Silver, D. (1989). How Black and Latino Community Organizations Respond to the AIDS Epidemic: A Case Study in One New York City Neighborhood. *AIDS Education and Prevention* 1:12-21.

Friedland, G.H., Saltzman, B., Vileno, J., Freeman, K., Schrager, L.K., and Klein, R.S. (1991). Survival Differences in Patients with AIDS. *Journal of Acquired Immune Deficiency Syndromes* 4(2):144-153.

Friedman, S.R., Des Jarlais, D.C., and Sterk, C.E. (1990). AIDS and the Social Relations of Intravenous Drug Users. *The Milbank Quarterly* 68:85-110.

Friedman, S., Sotheran, J.L., Abdul-Quader, A., Primm, B.J., Des Jarlais, D.C., Kleinman, P., Maugie, C., and Goldsmith, D.S. (1987). The AIDS Epidemic Among Blacks and Hispanics. *The Milbank Quarterly* 65(2):455-499.

Fromm-Reichmann, F. (196). *Principles of Intensive Psychotherapy.* Chicago: The University of Chicago Press.

Gasch, H., Poulson, D.M., and Fullilove, R.E. (1991). Shaping AIDS Education and Prevention Programs for African Americans, Amidst Community Decline. *Journal of Negro Education* 60(1):85-96.

Gilman, S.L. (1988). *Disease and Representation.* Ithaca: Cornell University Press.

Goffman, E. (1976). *Stigma: Notes on the Management of Spoiled Identity.* New York: Simon & Schuster, A Touchstone Book.

Goleman, Daniel. (1995). Early Violence Leaves Its Mark on the Brain. *The New York Times.* October 3.

Greaves, W. (1986). AIDS: No Time for Apathy. *Journal of the National Medical Association* 78:97-98.

Greaves, W.L. (1987). The Black Community. In *AIDS and the Law, A Guide for the Public.* (H.L. Dalton, S. Burris, and the Yale AIDS Law Project, eds.) New Haven and London: Yale University Press.

Gwinn, M., Pappaioanou, M., George, J.R., Hannon, W.H., Wasser, S.C., Redus, M.A., Hoff, R., Grady, G.F., Willoughby, A., Novello, A.C., et al. (1991). Prevalence of HIV Infection in Childbearing

Women in the United States: Surveillance Using Newborn Blood Samples. *Journal of the American Medical Association*, 1991; 265:1704-1708.

Haan, M., Kaplan, G.A., and Camacho, T. (1987). Poverty and Health: Prospective Evidence from the Alameda County Study. *American Journal Of Epidemiology* 125:989-998.

Hall, R.L., Wilder, D., Bodenroeder, P., and Hess, M. (1990). Assessment of AIDS Knowledge, Attitudes, Behaviors, and Risk Level of Northwestern American Indians. *American Journal of Public Health* 80(7):875-877.

Hamilton, J.D., Hartigan, P.M., Simberkoff, M.S., and the VA Cooperative Study Group, Department of Veterans Affairs. (1991). Early vs. Later Zidovudine Treatment of Symptomatic HIV infection. *Clinical Research* 39:216a.

Hart, B. (1992). Remarks to the Task Force on Child Abuse and Neglect. April.

Hayward, R.A., Bernard, A.M., Freeman, H.E., and Corey, R.C. (1991). Regular Sources of Ambulatory Care and Access to Health Services. *American Journal of Public Health* 81:434-438.

Hernandez, J.T. and Smith, F.J. (1991). Racial Targeting of AIDS Programs Reconsidered. *Journal of the National Medical Association* 83:17-21.

Hingson, R.W. and Strunin, L. (1990). Beliefs About AIDS, Use of Alcohol and Drugs, and Unprotected Sex Among Massachusetts adolescents. *American Journal of Public Health* 80(3):295-299.

Hoffman, L. (1981). *The Foundations of Family Therapy*, New York: Basic Books.

Hollis, F. and Woods, M.E. (1981). *Casework: A Psychosocial Therapy*. New York: Random House.

Holloway, M. (1994). Trends in Women's Health, A Global View. *Scientific Americus*. August: 27(2).

Holman, P.B., Jenkins, W.C., Gayle, J.A., Duncan, C., and Lindsey, B.K. (1991). Increasing the Involvement of National and Regional Racial and Ethnic Minority Organizations in HIV Information and Education. *Public Health Reports* 106(6):687-694.

Holtzman, D., Anderson, J.E., Kann, L., Arday, S.L., Truman, B.I., Kolbe, L.J. (1991). HIV Instruction, HIV Knowledge, and Drug

Injection Among High School Students in the United States. *American Journal of Public Health* 81(12):1596-1601.

Hoopes, J.L. and Stein, L.M. (1995). Identity Formation in the Adopted Adolescent, The Delaware Valley Study. Washington, DC: Child Welfare League of America.

Hops, H., Tildesley, E., Lichtenstein, E., Ary, D., and Sherman, L. (1990). Parent-adolescent Problem-Solving Interactions and Drug Use. *American Journal of Drug and Alcohol Abuse* 16:239-258.

Horney, K. (1967). *Feminine Psychology.* New York: W. W. Norton.

Jaynes, G.D. and Williams, R.M. Jr. (1989). A Common Destiny: Blacks and American Society. Washington, DC: National Academy Press.

Jewett, C.L. (1978). Adopting The Older Child. Boston, MA: Harvard Common Press.

Karon, J.M. and Berkelman, R.L. (1991). The Geographic and Ethnic Diversity of AIDS Incidence Trends in Homosexual/Bisexual Men in the United States. *Journal of Acquired Immune Deficiency Syndromes* 4:1179-1189.

Keith, S.N. (1990). Role of Minority Providers in Caring for the Underserved. *Journal of Health Care for the Poor and Underserved* 1:90-95.

Kellam, S.G., Brown, C.H., Rubin, B.R., and Ensminger, M.E. (1983). Paths Leading to Teenage Psychiatric Symptoms and Substance Use: Developmental Epidemiological Studies in Woodlawn. In S.B. Guze, F.J. Earls, and J.E. Barrett (eds.) *Childhood Psychopathology and Development.* New York: Raven, 17-51.

Kirk, D.H. (1964). *Shared Fate.* New York: Free Press.

Kluft, R.P. (1990). *Incest-Related Syndromes of Adult Psychopathology,* Washington, DC: American Psychiatric Press.

Koonin, L.M., Atrash, H.K., Lawson, H.W., and Smith, J.C. (1991). Maternal Mortality Surveillance, United States, 1979-1986. *Morbidity and Mortality Weekly Report Surveillance Summaries* 40(No. SS-1):1-13.

Kopp, C.B. (1983). Risk Factors in Development. In *Infancy and Developmental Psychology, 4th edition.* New York, John Wiley and Sons, 1081-1088.

Kraft, A.D., Palumbo, J., Mitchell D.L., Woods, P.K., Schmidt, A.W., and Tucker, N.G. (1985). Some Theoretical Considerations on Confidential Adoptions: Part III: The Adopted Child. *Child and Adolescence Social Work Journal*, vol. 2, 139-153.

Krainski K., Borkowsky W., and Bebenroth, B. (1988). Failure of Voluntary Testing for Human Immunodeficiency Virus to Identify Infected Parturient Women in a High-Risk Population. *New England Journal of Medicine*, 818:185.

Krieger, N. and Margo, G. (1990). Introduction: AIDS: The Politics of Survival. *International Journal of Health Services* 20(4):583-588.

Krueger, L.E., Wood, R.W., Diehr, P.H., and Maxwell, C.L. (1990). Poverty and HIV Seropositivity: The Poor Are More Likely To Be Infected. *AIDS* 4:811-814.

Landesman, S., Minkoff, H., Holman, S., MeCalla, S., and Sijin, O. (1987). Serosurvey of Human Immunodeficiency Virus Infection in Parturients: Implications for Human Immunodeficiency Virus Testing Programs of Pregnant Women. *Journal of the American Medical Association*, 258:2701-2703.

Lee, D.A. and Fong, K. (February/March, 1990). HIV/AIDS and the Asian and Pacific Islander Community. *SEICUS Report*.

Leman, N. (December, 1991). *The Atlantic Monthly*, 96-110.

Levine, S. (1982). *Who Dies?* New York: Anchor Books.

Levine, C. and Dubler, N.N. (1990). Uncertain Risks and Bitter Realities: The Reproductive Choices of HIV-infected Women. *The Milbank Quarterly* 68:321-351.

Lewes, K. (1988). *The Psychoanalytic Theory of Male Homosexuality*, New York: Simon & Schuster.

Lewis, S.H., Reynolds-Kahler, C., Fox, H.E., and Nelson, J.A. (1990). HIV-1 in Trophoblastic and Villous Hofbauer Cells, and Haematological Precursors in Eight-Week Fetuses. *Lancet* 335:565-568.

Lindan, C.P., Hearst, N., Singleton, J.A., Tractenberg, A.I., Riordan, N.M., Tokagawa, D.A., and Chu, G.S. (1990). Underreporting of Minority AIDS Deaths in San Francisco Bay Area, 1985-1986. *Public Health Reports* 105(4):400-404.

Lindholm, B.W. and Touliatos, J. (1980). Psychological Adjustment of Adopted and Nonadopted Children. *Psychological Reports*, vol. 46, 307-310.

Links, Paul S. (1990). *Family Environment and Borderline Personality Disorder*, Washington, DC: American Psychiatric Press.

Lundstrom, M. and Sharpe, R. (1990). It's Easy to Kill a Child. *USA Today*. December 17.

March of Dimes. (1992).

Marin, B.V. and Marin, G. (1992). Predictions of Condom Accessibility Among Hispanics in San Francisco. *American Journal of Public Health* 82:592-595.

Martin, K. (1990). A Shared Responsibility: A Native Person with AIDS and His Community. *Seasons*, Summer.

Mays, V.M. and Cochran, S.D. (1987). Issues in the Perception of AIDS Risk and Risk Reduction Activities by Black and Hispanic/Latina Women. *American Psychologist* 40:949-957.

McBride, D. (1991). *From TB to AIDS: Epidemics Among Urban Blacks Since 1900*. Albany, NY: State University of New York Press.

McCord, C. and Freeman, H.P. (1990). Excess Mortality in Harlem. *New England Journal of Medicine* 322:173-177.

McGoldrick, M. and Pearce, J.K. (1984). *Ethnicity and Family Therapy*, New York: Guilford Press.

McNeil, J.G., Brundage, J.F., Gardner, L.I., Wann, Z.F., Renzullo, P.O., Redfield, R.A., Burke, D.S., and Miller, R.N. (1991). HIV Seroconversion Among Young Adults in the U.S. Army, 1985 to 1989. *Journal of the American Medical Association,* 265(13):1709-1714.

Melina, L.R. (1986). *Raising Adopted Children: A Manual for Adoptive Parents*. New York: Harper and Row.

Michaels, D. and Levine, C. (July, 1992a). Projections of the Number of motherless Youth Orphaned by AIDS in the United States. Presented at the VIII International Conference on AIDS. Amsterdam.

Michaels D. and Levine C. (1992b). Estimates of the Number of Motherless Youth Orphaned by AIDS in the United States. *Journal of the American Medical Association*, 268:3461.

Miller, J.B. (1986). *Toward a New Psychology of Women.* Boston: Beacon Press.

Miller, S.M. (1987). Race in the Health of America. *The Milbank Quarterly* 65(2):500-531.

Millet, K. (1970). *Sexual Politics.* New York: Equinox.

Minuchin, S. (1974). *Families and Family Therapy.* Cambridge: Harvard University Press.

Mofenson, L.M. and Wolinsky, S.M. (1994). Current Insights Regarding Vertical Transmission. In Pizzo, P.A. and C.M. Wilfert (eds.), *Pediatric HIV Disease: The Challenge of HIV Infection in Infants, Children, and Adolescents*, 2nd ed. Baltimore: Williams & Wilkins, 179-203.

Moore, R.D., Hidalgo, J., Fugland, B.W., and Chaisson, R.E. (1991). Zidovudine and the Natural History of the Acquired Immunodeficiency Syndrome. *New England Journal of Medicine* 324:1412-1415.

Morgan, R. (1984). *Sisterhood Is Global.* New York: Anchor/Doubleday.

Myers, M.T. Jr. (1992). The African American Experience with HIV Disease. *Focus* 7:1-4.

National Association of People with AIDS. (1992). HIV in America: A Profile of the Challenges Facing Americans Living with HIV. Washington, DC: National Association of People with AIDS.

National Center for Health Statistics. U.S. Department of Health and Human Services.

National Commission on AIDS. (1992). Washington, DC, December.

National Council of La Raza. (July, 1991). AIDS in the Hispanic Community: An Update. Washington, DC: National Council of La Raza.

National Council of La Raza. (March, 1992). Hispanics and Health Insurance Volume 1: Status. Washington, DC: National Council of La Raza.

National Institute of Allergy and Infectious Diseases (NIAID), reported in the December 28 (AU supply date). *Journal of the American Medical Association.*

National Minority AIDS Council. (March, 1992). The Impact of HIV on Communities of Color: A Blueprint for the Nineties. Washington, DC: National Minority AIDS Council.

Nelkin, D. and Gilman, S.L. (1988). Placing Blame for Devastating Disease. *Social Research* 55:362-378.

New York State Department of Health. (July 10, 1992). *Pediatric HIV Continuum of Care Study Final Report*. Albany, NY: AIDS Institute.

Nickens, H.W. (1990). AIDS Among Blacks in the 1990s. *Journal of the National Medical Association* 82:239-242.

Nickens, H.W. (1991). The Health Status of Minority Populations in the United States. *Western Journal of Medicine* 155:27-32.

Nickman, S.L. (1985). Losses in Adoption: The Need for Dialogue. *The Psychoanalytic Study of the Child*, vol. 40, 365-397.

O'Donnell, J. and Jones, J. (1968). Diffusion of Intravenous Techniques Among Narcotic Addicts in the U.S. *Journal of Health and Social Behavior* 9:120-130.

Parens, H. (1987). *Aggression in Our Children: Coping with It Constructively*. New Jersey: Jason Aronson, Inc.

Peterson, J.L. and Marin G. (1988). Issues in the Prevention of AIDS Among Black and Hispanic Men. *American Psychologist* 43:871-877.

Ports, S.T. and Banzhaf, M. (1990). *Many Cultures, Many Approaches. Women, AIDS, and Activism*. New York: ACTUP/ New York Women and AIDS Book Group.

Praeger, J. (1982). American Racial Ideology as Collective Representation. *Ethnic and Racial Studies* 5:99-119.

Press Release. (1994). National Institutes of Health, National Institute of Allergy and Infectious Diseases, February 20.

Public Health Service (PHS). (1990). *Healthy People 2000: National Health Promotion and Disease Prevention Objectives*. Washington, DC: US Government Printing Office.

Rich, A. (1976). *Of Woman Born: Motherhood as Experience and Institution*. New York: W. W. Norton.

Rieder, I. and Ruppelt, P. (1988). *AIDS: The Women*. San Francisco: Cleis Press.

Rogers, M.F. and Williams, W.W. (1987). AIDS in Blacks and Hispanics: Implications for Prevention. *Issues in Science and Technology* Spring: 89-94.

Rogers, M.F., Ou, C.Y., Rayfield, M., Thomas, P.A., Schoenbaum, E.E., Abrams, E., Krasinski, K., Selwyn, P.A., Moore, J., Kaul, A., et al. (1989). Use of the Polymerase Chain Reaction for Early Detection of the Proviral Sequences of Human Immunodeficiency Virus in Infants Born to Seropositive Mothers. *New England Journal of Medicine*, 320:1649-1654.

Rosenthal, E. (1990). Abortions Often Denied to Women with AIDS Virus. *The New York Times*. October 23.

Rouzioux, C., Costagliola, D., Burgard, M., Blanche, S., Mayaux, M.J., Griscelli, C., and Valleron, A.J. (1993). Timing of Mother-to-Child HIV-1 Transmission Depends on Maternal Status. *HIV Disease* 7 (Supplement 2): 549-552.

Rowell, R.M. (February/March, 1990). Native Americans, Stereotypes and HIV/AIDS: Our Continuing Struggle for survival. *SEICUS Report,* 9-15.

Rush, A.G. (1990). Substance Abuse and HIV in Native Communities. *Seasons,* Fall.

Rushton, J.P. and Bogaert, A.F. (1989). Population Differences in Susceptibility to AIDS: An Evolutionary Analysis. *Social Science and Medicine* 28(12):1211-1220.

Russell, D.E.H. (1986). *The Secret Trauma: Incest in the Lives of Girls and Women*, New York: Basic Books.

Ryder, R.W., Nsa, W., Hassig, S.E. Behets, F., Rayfield, M., Ekungola, B., Nelson, A.M., Mulenda, U., Francis, H., Mwandagalirwa, K., et al. (1989). Perinatal Transmission of the Human Immunodeficiency Virus Type I to Infants of Seropositive Women in Zaire. *New England Journal of Medicine* 320:1637-1642.

Sants, H.J. (1964). Genealogical Bewilderment in Children with Substitute Parents. *British Journal of Medical Psychology*, vol. 37, 133-141.

Scarlatti, G., Albert, J., Rossi, P., Hodara, V., Biraghi, P., Muggiasca, L. and Fenyö, E.M. (1993). Mother-to-Child Transmission of Human Immunodeficiency Virus Type 1: Correlation with Neutralizing Antibodies Against Primary Isolates. *Journal of Infectious Diseases* 168:207-210.

Schecter, M.D., Carlson, P.V., Simmons, J.Q., III, and Work, H.H. (1964). Emotional Problems in the Adoptee. *Archives of General Psychiatry*, vol. 10,109-118.

Schoenbaum, E.E., Hartel, D., Selwyn, P.A., Klein, R.S., Davenny, K., Rogers, M., Feiner, C., Friedland, G. (1989). Risk Factors for Human Immunodeficiency Virus Infection in Intravenous Drug Users. *The New England Journal of Medicine* 321(13):874-879.

Selik, R.M., Castro, K.G., and Pappaioanou, M. (1988). Racial/Ethnic Differences in the Risk of AIDS in the United States. *American Journal of Public Health* 78:1539-1546.

Selik, R.M., Castro, K.G., Pappaioanou, M., and Buehler, J.W. (1989). Birthplace and the Risk of AIDS Among Hispanics in the U.S. *American Journal of Public Health* 79:836-839.

Senate Judiciary Hearings. (1990). Violence Against Women Act.

Serrill, M.S. (1993). Defiling the Children. *Time* June 21.

Shayne, V.T. and Kaplan, B.J. (1991). Double Victims: Poor Women and AIDS. *Women and Health* 17:21-37.

Sharpe, R. and Lundstrom, M. (1991). Failure to Investigate Suspicious Deaths of Children is Criminal. *USA Today.* April 11.

Short, P.F., Cornelius, L.J., and Goldstone, D.E. (1990). Health Insurance of Minorities in the United States. *Journal of Health Care for the Poor and Underserved* 1:9-24.

Singer, M., Flores, C., Davison, L., Burke, G., Castillo, Z. (1990). SIDA: The Economic, Social, and Cultural Context of AIDS Among Latinos. *Medical Anthropology Quarterly* 4:72-114.

Smith, D.K. (1992). HIV, Disease as a Cause of Death for African-Americans: 1987-1991. *Journal of the National Medical Association* 6(84):481-487.

Smith, M. (1991). Zidovudine: Does It Work for Everyone? *Journal of the American Medical Association* 266:2750-2751.

Smith, J. and Miroff, F. (1987). *You're Our Child: The Adoption Experience.* Lanham, MD: Madison Books.

Smolowe, J. (1994). When Violence Hits Home. *Time.* July 1.

Sontag, S. (1977). *Illness as Metaphor.* New York: Vintage Book.

Sontag, S. (1989). *AIDS and Its Metaphors.* New York: Farrar, Straus and Giroux.

Speech given June 25, 1994, New York University, New York, New York.

St. Louis, M.E., Conway, G.A., Hayman, C.R., Miller, C., Petersen, L.R., and Dondero, T.J. (1991). Human Immunodeficiency Virus Infection in Disadvantaged Adolescents: Findings from the U.S. Job Corps. *Journal of the American Medical Association* 266(17): 2387-2391.

St. Louis, M.E., Kamenga, M., Brown, C., Nelson, A.M., Manzila, T., Batter, V., Behets, F., Kabagabo, U., Ryder, R.W., Oxtoby, M. et al.

(1993). Risk for Perinatal HIV-1 Transmission According to Maternal Immunologic, Virologic, and Placental Factors. *Journal of the American Medical Association* 269:2853-2859.

Starr, P. (1982). *The Social Transformation of American Medicine.* New York: Basic Books.

Steinem, G. (1992). *Revolution from Within.* Boston: Little, Brown & Company.

Storr, A. (1980). *The Art of Psychotherapy.* New York: Methuen.

Stroebe, W. and Stroebe, M.S. (1987). *Bereavement and Health,* New York: Cambridge University Press.

Surgeon General. (1995). United States.

Surgeon General Antonia Nobvello. As quoted in *Domestic Violence: Battered Women.* Publication of the Reference Department of the Cambridge Public Library, Cambridge, MA.

Tardiff, K., Marzuk, P.M., Leon, A.C., Hirsch, C.S., Stajie, M., Portera, L., and Hartwell, N. (1994). Homicide in New York City: Cocaine Use and Firearms. *Journal of the American Medical Association* 272:43-46.

Thomas, S.B. and Quinn, S.C. (1992). The Tuskeegee Syphilis Study, 1932 to 1972: Implications for HIV Education and AIDS Risk Education Programs in the Black Community. *American Journal of Public Health* 81(11):1498-1505.

Toufexis, A. (1992). When Kids Kill Abusive Parents. *Time* November 23.

Tuchman, B. (1978). *A Distant Mirror.* New York: Knopf.

Turner, F.J. (1976). *Differential Diagnosis and Treatment in Social Work.* New York: The Free Press.

Turner, F.J. (1986). *Social Work Treatment.* New York: The Free Press.

Uniform Crime Reports. (1990). Federal Bureau of Investigation.

Uniform Crime Reports. (1991). Federal Bureau of Investigation.

United Nations. (1989). The General Assembly, Convention on the Rights of the Child, November.

U.S. Department of Justice. (1983). Bureau of Justice Statistics, Washington, DC, October.

U.S. Senate Committee on the Judiciary. (1991). Violence Against Women: Victims of the System.

Valdiserri, R.O., West, G.R., Moore, M., Darrow, W.W., and Hinman, A.R. (1992). Structuring HIV Prevention Service Delivery

Systems on the Basis of Social Science Theory. *Journal of Community Health* 17:259-269.

Van Biema, D. (1993). Robbing the Innocents. *Time* December 29.

Van Biema, D. (1994). Mother and Child Reunion. *Time* January 24.

Waldinger, R.J. and Gunderson, J.G. (1987). *Effective Psychotherapy with Borderline Patients*. Washington, DC: American Psychiatric Press.

Wallace, R. (1990). Urban Decertification, Public Health, and Public Order: "Planned Shrinkage," Violent Death, Substance Abuse and AIDS in The Bronx. *Social Science and Medicine* 31(7):801-813.

Watters, J.K. and Lewis, D.K. (1990). HIV Infection, Race, and Drug-treatment History. *AIDS* 4(7):697-702.

Weissman, J.S., Stern, R., Fielding, S.L., and Epstein, A.M. (1991). Delayed Access to Health Care: Risk Factors, Reasons, and Consequences. *Annals of Internal Medicine* 114(4):325-331.

Wieder, H. (1977). On Being Told of Adoption. *Psychoanalytic Quarterly* 1-22.

Wilkinson, D.Y. and King, G. (1987). Conceptual and Methodological Issues in the Use of Race as a Variable: Policy Implication. *The Milbank Quarterly* 65:56-71.

Winkler, R.C., Brown, D.W., Von Keppel, M., and Blanchard, A. (1988). *Clinical Practice in Adoption*. New York: Pergamon Press, Inc.

Wolstein, B. (1988). *Essential Papers on Countertransference*. New York: New York University Press.

World Health Organization. (1995). Global Programme on AIDS, January.

Wyatt, G.E. (1991). Examining Ethnicity Versus Race in AIDS Related Sex Research. *Social Science and Medicine* 33(1):37-45.

Yalom, I.D. (1975). *The Theory and Practice of Group Psychotherapy*. New York: Basic Books.

Yalom, I.D. (1990). *Love's Executioner: Tales of Psychotherapy*. New York: Basic Books

Youth Bill of Rights. (1989). National Child Rights Alliance, September.

Zuk, G.H. and Boszormenyi-Nagy, I. (1969). *Family Therapy and Disturbed Families*. Palo Alto: Science and Behavior Books.

Index

Abandonment of children, 27-29
Abuse. *See* Child abuse; Domestic
 Violence; Violence
Acquired immune deficiency
 syndrome (AIDS). *See* HIV
 (human immunodeficiency
 virus) disease
ACT UP (AIDS Committee
 to Unleash Power), 105-106
Addiction, 124-125
Adolescents and HIV prevention, 20.
 See also Children
Adoption. *See also* Family; Foster
 care; Orphaned children
 and family, redefinition of, 29-30
 foster care and obstructions to, 30
 personal histories
 Julia and Jamal, 77-84
 Renee and Toni, 43-52
 Theiren, Stephen, Lawrence,
 and Billy, 98-107,109-120
 separation anxiety in children,
 112-113,119-120
 special-needs children and, 29-30
Adoption Assistance and Child
 Welfare Act (1980), 30
Africa, HIV incidence in, 9-10
African Americans
 adoptions by, personal histories,
 83-84,99-107
 domestic violence and, 132
 and family, changing nature
 of, 86,87,88,104,105
 and HIV disease, 2,3,18,20,23-25
 kidnapping of, 38
 Kwanza, 53-54
 population statistics of, 88
 Santería, 73-75

African Americans *(continued)*
 violence against, 139-140
 violent crime and drug use
 and, 122-124
AIDS (acquired immune deficiency
 syndrome). *See* HIV (human
 immunodeficiency virus)
 disease
AIDS Committee to Unleash Power
 (ACT UP), 105-106
Alaskan Natives. *See* American
 Indians
Alcohol consumption. *See also* Drug
 use
 addictiveness of, 125
 depression and, 6
 domestic violence and, 130
 gender differences in, 122
 prevalence of, 126,127-128
American Indians
 domestic violence and, 132
 HIV incidence in, 3,18,23,24,25
American Society for the Prevention
 of Cruelty to Animals
 (ASPCA), 53
American Society for the Prevention
 of Cruelty to Children
 (ASPCC), 53
Angel (personal history), 59-75
Anger, children and, 5
Animal welfare and shelters, 53,128
Anonymous, 4,111
Asian Americans
 domestic violence and, 132
 HIV incidence in, 3,18,20,23,
 24,25
 population statistics of, 88

ASPCA (American Society
      for the Prevention of Cruelty
      to Animals), 53
AZT (zidovudine), prenatal
      transmission and, 19-20

Baldwin, James, 104
Barbiturates, 125
Basta!, 90
Battered child-syndrome, 33. *See
      also* Child abuse
Battering. *See* Domestic violence
Bensonhurst, 139-140,144
Billy (personal history), 98-107,
      109-120
Birth rates, 87
Bisexual men. *See also* Gay men;
      Lesbians
   as fathers, 88
   HIV incidence in, 10,13
Blood products, 13,14
Boarder babies, 27,29
Bottoms, Sharon, 89
Breastfeeding, 18,19
Bronx, The, 72,77-78

Carnarsie people, 140
Center Kids, *ix*,106-107
Cervical cancer, 16-17
Cheyney State University, 104-105
Child abuse
   adult criminality and, 128-129
   ages of victims, 132,135
   causes of, 32-33,34-35
   defined, 30
   effects and symptoms of, 30-32,
      33,35-36,128-129
   forms of, 31-32,33-35,37,
      38-40,131
   parricide and, 37,38
   perpetrators of, 33,34-35,36,37,
      129,134

Child abuse *(continued)*
   prevention of and intervention
      in, 28-29,30,35,36-37,
      40-41,53
   race/ethnicity of victims, 132
   reporting of, 30
   sexual abuse, 32,35-40,93,134,135
Child Abuse Prevention
      and Treatment Act (1974), 35
Child pornography, 32,39
Child prostitution, 32,38-40
Child Welfare Administration (New
      York City), 107
Children. *See also* Men; Women
   abandonment of, 27-29,112-113,
      119-120
   abuse of. *See* Child abuse
   adoption of. *See* Adoption
   anger and, 5
   behavior as barometer of feelings,
      112-113,119-120,144-145
   boarder babies, 27,29
   death and. *See* Death
   family and. *See* Family
   in foster care. *See* Foster care
   guilt and, 6
   and HIV disease
      geographic distribution of, 22
      incidence of, 2,3,10,18,19
      transmission of, 18-20
   in medieval society, 27-28
   as orphans. *See* Orphaned children
   parricide and, 37-38
   rights of, 40-41
   and school. *See* School
   separation anxiety of, 112-113,
      119-120
   sibling rivalry, personal history,
      116-119
Christopher Street Gay Pride March,
      95
Cigarettes, 126,127,128
Clifford, Jim, 90

Women. *See also* Lesbians; Men
  abuse of. *See* Domestic violence
  birth rates, 87
  drug use by
    abandonment of children
      and, 27
    causes of, 121-122
    and homicide of, 122-124
    patterns of, 29
    in pregnancy, 3,27,29,127-128
    prevalence of, 124,125-128
  and family. *See* Family
  gay men's support of, 91-92,94
  and HIV disease
    characteristics of disease, 16-17
    death rates, 2,13,16
    incidence of, 1-2,13,20-21,
      25,136
    modes of infection, 2,21

Women, and HIV disease
  (continued)
    obstacles to treatment
      of, 16,135-136
  as homicide victims, 122-124
  pregnancy
    battering during, 128,133-134
    drug use during, 3,27,29,
      127-128
    HIV transmission during,
      2,18-20
  roles of, as changing, 87-88
  status of, and health care, 16,
    17-18,136
  substance use by, 2-3
Workplace problems, and domestic
  violence, 135

Zidovudine (AZT), 19-20